MW00681029

FROM DARKNESS INTO LIGHT

The Shana Campbell Story

Deacon Kevin R. Carges

Wild About Words Publishing
Rochester, NY 2018

To purchase additional copies, contact the author at deaconkevin@yahoo.com or write to the author at 330 S. Main St, Canandaigua, NY 14424

To contact Wild About Words Publishing, contact Jane Sutter Brandt at jane@suttermedia.net.

ISBN 978-1-7329881-0-1

Cover design: Wendy Glaess

Profits from the sale of this book are dedicated to a scholarship fund for Shana Campbell.

Dedicated to the parish community of
Our Lady of Peace in Geneva, New York.
Thank you for your support in so many ways,
I am blessed.

Ephesians 5:8-9

There was a time when you were darkness, but now you are a light in the Lord. Well then, live as children of light. Light produces every kind of goodness and justice and truth.

Table of Contents

Foreword

In early July of 1979, shortly after my installation as Bishop of Rochester, I ran in the Chemung Canal Elmirathon. During the race, a high school student named Kevin Carges drew up beside me and kindly made himself known to me. He wanted to welcome his new bishop. He was also eager for me to know that Father Bernie Carges, a friend of mine from seminary days at Saint Bernard's in Rochester, was his uncle.

After that race, I told Bernie about my delightful encounter with his nephew. Between that conversation and the time of his death, Bernie kept me in touch with his nephew's growth into adulthood. During the 1979 race and in those conversations with his uncle, I became aware that Kevin was a gifted and generous young man who would do good things in his life.

Given his lively faith and his desire to serve others, it was no surprise to me that Kevin responded to God's call to seek ordination as a permanent deacon for service in the Diocese of Rochester. I had the privilege of ordaining him in 2005.

Little did I imagine that one day I would be recommending that you read Kevin's latest book, *From Darkness Into Light: The Shana Campbell Story.*

This is the story of a beautiful, strong Jamaican girl who at a young age was physically and emotionally brutalized by her father. It's hard to imagine that anyone reading her story would not be deeply moved by her courage or wonder how she has maintained such a positive and open spirit. What an example she is to all of us of how the human spirit can grow, even flourish, in the midst of profound suffering.

This book is also a beautiful reminder of our baptismal call to serve others in the name of the Lord. Deacon Kevin Carges lives that call now as a permanent deacon, and he does it with courage and humility. He is unafraid to launch into the deep, cast a net and trust the Lord to bring to fruition his efforts on behalf of others. He is also unafraid to ask for help, even to challenge others to unite in common effort for those in need.

The story brings me back to memories of the young guy I met in Elmira 37 years ago, and it invites me to prayer and reflection on how God calls us all to new life and growth all the days of our lives.

From Darkness To Light: the Shana Campbell Story tells a powerful and moving story. I recommend it to you with confidence that reading it will make a difference in your life.

Matthew H. Clark
Bishop Emeritus, Diocese of Rochester, New York

A JAMAICAN ROAD LEADS TO SHANA CAMPBELL

In 2010 I founded a volunteer group called Eight 4 World Hope— an odd name, I know. It was with some friends of mine with whom I had graduated from St. John Fisher College, class of '84. It had eight members starting out: six of my friends from college, myself, and of course the leader of the whole group, Jesus Christ, who we pray guides our actions—after all, this is His work.

Our goal was to help those in need through education in the developing world. I'd seen a lot of difficult things by this time in my life after spending time in Jamaica, Haiti and Nicaragua. A couple of years later I would visit Kenya. Eight 4 World Hope's first project was a small school called Sacred Heart Basic School in Concord, Jamaica, near the north coast.

The school was infested with mold and bats. The Ministry of Education in Jamaica had ordered it to be closed due to the unsafe conditions. Oftentimes in Jamaica, the community is responsible for its own schools, and if they're in a poor section of the country, the residents have little access to resources to fix the various problems that arise.

After hearing the story of the school, I flew down to Jamaica with my daughter Allison to see if the need was indeed real and worth our efforts. It was only my second time to Jamaica, the first being in 2006, a trip that changed me forever. Seeing the severe poverty of this paradise island touched my heart as nothing had before.

I had worked with many people in the upstate New York area through food cupboards, overnight shelters and soup kitchens. I had heard many stories of suffering and sadness. They always touched my heart, but I also knew there was somewhere to go for help. Jamaica was very different; the suffering was far more intense and there was nowhere to go for help. People were literally left on their own to survive often times.

The stories not only touched my heart, but grabbed and shook it within me. So many thousands of people lived in makeshift homes of wood and sheet metal, barely held together by a few nails. Worse yet were those I met living in landfills with only a cardboard box to call home. Seeing a mother having to choose between food for her hungry children or medicine for a sick child hurt me deeply.

Little did I know the journey God was planning for me in 2006 when the opportunity arose to serve those in need in a developing country. By 2010, when Eight 4 World Hope came together with a specific purpose, I had a better understanding of how God wanted to use me as His vessel and how it would lead me to a young girl named Shana Kay Campbell in January 2015.

By May 2013, Eight 4 World Hope was dedicating its third project, a basic school in McCook Pen (about 27 kilometers west of Kingston), and visiting potential new projects. This was such a blessing for me as McCook Pen Basic School was the worst situation I had come across in Jamaica thus far. What our group had been able to accomplish was far beyond my dreams.

You can see very clearly from the pictures the difference we can make when we come together. The kitchen is a very important part of a school because the schools provide a meal to the children, sometimes their only meal for the day. Beans and rice are always on the menu and occasionally, when times are good, there is some chicken. Eight 4 World Hope raised $58,000 to build a new school that included three classrooms and a kitchen, flush toilets with a septic system, a sickbay, a community room, as well as a computer lab with six computers. The story made the front page of the national newspaper in Jamaica, The Observer, as it was such a benefit for the community of McCook Pen.

Dignitaries from all over Jamaica came out for the dedication as we celebrated the new school.

The next day we visited Planters All Age School in Old Harbor, Jamaica, about 37 kilometers west of Kingston. The school had approximately 240 students from ages 3 to15. The school had pit latrines built in 1968 that were in dire need of being replaced. Again, the Ministry of Education in Jamaica was threatening to close the school due to the unsafe conditions of the aging latrines.

One reason Jamaica is closing the schools rather than repairing them is that the country is in the midst of a severe economic hardship due to the global recession and inflation of the Jamaican dollar. Fifteen percent of the country's GDP comes from remissions, that is, money that Jamaicans who have left the country send to family members still in Jamaica. Tourism is the number three source of income, trailing the mining of bentonite, which is used in the manufacture of aluminum. Some reports estimated that remissions had fallen to five percent due to the recession. Jamaicans abroad simply didn't have the extra money to send back to their families.

As I walked around the school to assess the need, I met Sharon Campbell Danvers, the school's principal. She had recently come to the school to help keep it open. She was certainly a woman of faith and strong belief who had that special gift of being able to rally people around her to make the impossible possible.

Her spirit and determination really excited me. She's one of those people you want to work with, because you know that together you will accomplish great things. After seeing the need at the school and meeting Sharon and her staff, the board members of Eight 4 World Hope decided that Planter All Age School would be our fourth project. Our goal was to raise $15,000 to build new bathrooms for the students, ensuring that the school would remain open and the 200-plus students would continue to receive an education. Little did I know then that Sharon Campbell Danvers would become a significant person within my life over the coming years.

I returned to Jamaica in May 2014 to celebrate the dedication of the new bathroom facility with the community of Old Harbor and Planters All Age School. When we arrived at the school, I learned that Sharon was no longer the principal of the school as she had been asked to take on a larger project in desperate need. She was there for the dedication and gave a wonderful thank-you speech to our group and others who had made the new bathrooms possible.

Having completed the new sanitation project and a school expansion at St. Theresa's, another school in Mt. Friendship, Jamaica, it was time to look at some new potential projects - for the group. Food for the Poor (FFP) was our guide and partner, acting as my eyes and ears on the ground in Jamaica. People throughout Jamaica reach out to FFP for help and FFP tries to assist them with their various needs. They are a wonderful organization serving in 17 countries in the Caribbean and Latin America.

To celebrate the fiftieth anniversary of Jamaican independence, FFP had initiated an aggressive goal of building fifty new schools in Jamaica over the next couple years. Our group was part of this effort, trying to ensure children got the education they needed in hopes of lifting themselves out of the poverty they were born into.

That week we toured a few potential projects just outside of Kingston, the Jamaican capital, including Davis Primary School, about four or five miles away from Planter's All Age School.

I remember getting off the bus at Davis Primary School. It was built in 1973 for 200 children but, due to the community growing and lack of schools in the area, - more than 700 children were now packed into the building, with an additional 200 children on a waiting list. The school needed to be expanded and repaired extensively. The sanitation was so bad that the school was closed on various days due to sewage seeping up to the surface of the ground. Overcrowding was the underlying problem: There were too many children for such a small facility, yet the teachers were so committed to the children that they accepted every child they could fit in the door.

The rooms were divided into sections by chalkboards so as to create "separate" classrooms. Children were packed into the rooms, - even sitting on the floor when there were no more chairs. Children had to crawl under desks to reach the back rows as desks and chairs took up all the space in order to accommodate as many children as possible.

It was a school in big trouble, and hope was fading that it could be saved from closure. Sadly, the Jamaican government could offer little; the school needed too much work to make it safe for the children. The community rallied trying to raise-funds for their school, but being one of the poorer communities in Jamaica, they had only been

able to raise about $2,000 over the last few years. As I was told about all the needs, I turned to the back page of the new school proposal to see the bottom line. My heart broke as I saw that the amount needed was over $155,000, almost three times as much as our biggest project to date and almost twice of what we had raised over three years.

Our biggest project had been a $58,000 new school building for McCook Pen Basic School. It took our small group longer to raise such a large amount, but the original school was in such bad shape that we couldn't say no.

It was an intimidating amount for Eight 4 World Hope. I looked up at the school and said to myself, "How, God?" I wondered why Food for the Poor would even bring me here. It was too big a project but since we were here, I figured we might as well go see everything.

I was introduced to the principal, who was, believe it or not, Sharon Campbell Danvers! I smiled when I saw her and learned that the Ministry of Education had begged her to come here and take on the huge project of saving this school. She had done such a wonderful job at Planters All Age School, and now Davis Primary School needed her badly.

Sharon told me that she hadn't accepted the job right away. She prayed about it and it was only through prayer that she finally accepted the job, feeling that it was what God was asking of her. I laughed to myself as she told me, because the only reason I was even in Jamaica trying to help with the schools was because I felt God was asking me to do this.

I gave her a hug and told her that after what I had seen her do at the last school, I had no doubts that she would succeed. She just laughed and said, "I need help."

All I could say was, "Let's go take a look." Meanwhile, I thought, "I don't think we are the group to do it, it is just too big."

The students had the day off for a holiday so it was hard to judge what 737 children packed into a school built for 200 would look like as I walked through. Each classroom was packed with chairs and desks. It didn't take long to see how much work needed to be done for repairs, let alone expanding the school to hold up to-1,000 children. It was a big job.

As we toured the building, Sharon had a few students with her, including her daughters, and they demonstrated getting in and out of their desks each day. Some of the teachers showed up to greet us and tell us about how committed they were to these children and how much they needed help.

The love Sharon and her staff had for the children was so clear, it really touched my heart. As I walked through the buildings and classrooms, all I could think about was how much work needed to be done, and how small a group we were. How could we raise $155,000 and how long would it take us to do that? Our previous five projects didn't even add up to $155,000, and we had been doing this now for four years. These children couldn't wait that long, they needed help now.

I wished I were rich, I wished I could just come in and

save the day, but that wasn't a gift God had given me. If I was going to help, it was going to be hard and a lot of work, maybe too much. I was filled with doubt and apprehension. Our group of twenty people that I had brought to Jamaica with me eventually broke up and floated around the school taking things in on their own. As I walked into the various rooms, I eventually came to one that was large but separated by three or four chalkboards cutting through it to create an additional two classrooms. I was about ten steps in when I saw some writing on one of the chalkboards in pink chalk—it stuck out so much that you couldn't ignore it. I figured it was something the teacher had written for her students, a homework assignment or math equation, but as I walked towards it I saw it was a Biblical quotation, Philippians 4:13: "I can do all things through Christ who strengthens me."

I stood there just reading it over and over, letting it sink in. I began to feel foolish as I thought about my fears and reservations. I was so wrapped up in myself and self-doubt that I forgot that this isn't about me at all, but that this is God's work. It was like Jesus Christ, the head of our group, was slapping me in the head to remind me: "Hey,

I am doing this work through you and your friends. I will provide and give you the strength you need for this work. Have faith."

Lucky for me, seeing this quotation turned everything around. Yes, this was God's work, I must have faith and trust. Fortunately, my good friend, Tom D'Amico, was on this trip with me. Tom was then President of Eight 4 World Hope and someone on whom I really relied. He is the perfect complement for me as I tend to be pretty emotional, and he is a solid business leader with great vision and sound business sense. I was sure he understood the scope of this project far better than I did, and if he felt we could do it somehow, I would believe it also. As I read the line from Philippians one more time, my whole attitude changed. How could we not succeed with Sharon as principal of the school, Tom as president of the group, all the others back home, and, above all, Jesus leading the way?

I found Tom and asked him what he was thinking. The project was so big, but clearly Jesus was guiding him in the same direction as myself. Like me, Tom couldn't imagine how 700 kids were fitting into this small dilapidated school. But Tom was game to take it on, as was my wife, Jackie, who had joined me on the trip and had been my biggest supporter through everything. We agreed that we would go back home and suggest it to the other board members.

Now that I felt like we had a direction, I began to take some pictures to use for presentations back home. I happened to find myself walking around with a student named Shauna Lea, about 10 years old. She was one of Sharon's daughters and a great source of information, telling me all about the school, the students, and what life was like for her and the others.

Shauna Lea had a great smile and I really enjoyed talking with her. She represented the other 700 children whom I didn't get to meet that day but would later. It is one thing to know poverty exists, but it is another thing when poverty and disadvantage has a name. I went home a few days later, and Shauna Lea was with me in my heart representing the other 1,000 children who would eventually attend Davis Primary School once it expanded. I put a picture of Shauna Lea and me on my computer desktop as a reminder each day that I had work to do.

When Tom and I returned home, Tom actually led the cause to make Davis Primary School our next project, which wasn't a fight at all. The fact that Tom wanted to do it made me feel really confident. I just knew somehow God would provide, open doors, and do His work through our little group. The Eight 4 World Hope board decided that we would break the project into three pieces in hopes of getting construction moving faster and to address immediate needs. It is amazing to see God answer prayers through Eight 4 World Hope. He brought volunteers, donors, and everything together in a way that was somehow beyond even my hopes and dreams.

I was excited to be working with Sharon again as well; she inspired me. She fought so hard for her children in the school, wanting to give them all an education and loving each and every one of them with her whole heart. She was a true advocate for those children, and she motivated me with her desire to provide and give each of them an opportunity at a better life.

After it was agreed that Davis Primary School would be our next project, doors seemed to open up to us even wider. A couple years prior, I had written a book called God Took My Hand, and a copy of it fell into the right hands at the main office of the Roman Catholic Diocese of Rochester, New York. Father Robert Bradler, who headed the Propagation of Faith office there, read my book and called me. He invited me to apply to be a missionary preacher within our diocese. This would allow me to share the Eight 4 World Hope story at a church each year and have a collection taken up to support the organization. It was a real honor as more than 350 applications are submitted each year from all over the world, but only thirty or so are accepted. I went through the application process and was accepted to preach that July at St. Mary's Church in Canandaigua and St. Mary of the Lakes in Watkins Glen and Odessa, all in Western New York. I was able to raise about $10,000.

Over the course of that year, we hosted our first golf tournament, did various talks to service organizations and church groups, begged and pleaded through social networks, and even became the focus of a college course at St. John Fisher College, as I worked with some students spreading the word about Jamaica's needs and our group. After our annual Christmas appeal, we had raised the money for phase one of the project in only nine months, about $47,000.

Over the course of these nine months, I was blessed to get to know Sharon much better. We found each other on Facebook and exchanged emails, which helped me raise the funds much quicker as she shared photos and stories of the children and life back at Davis Primary School. I would, in turn, share them with others. As people heard the story and saw the pictures of the children, more and more began to understand the impact our work was having. One of my goals in establishing this group back in 2010 was to connect people here with people there, wherever "there" may be. I wanted donors to see where their dollars went, the people they were helping, and, of course, the before-and-after photos, so we could all share in the satisfaction of our efforts.

With Sharon's pictures and stories, it was clear that what had developed was exactly my hope of two communities becoming one family in a truer sense. While we raised money, Davis School's students and administrators shared themselves with us, which inspired both our action and God's work coming to fruition. I also came to know Sharon as a woman of deep faith, so much so that she helped me in my own faith in times of struggle as we worked together making the school a better place. Working together had become a partnership of, not only mutual respect and admiration, but also a great friendship.

In January 2015, I emailed Sharon to tell her the good news that we had raised the money needed for phase one of the project. We would build a new building of classrooms as well as repair various issues at the original school building. I was so excited for the children—"my children" as I refer to them—all 737 of them at the Davis Primary School. All I could do was give thanks to God for His guidance all along the way. It was clearly God in action working through so many and, to be a small part of it, was a blessing beyond words.

From Tragedy to Hope For Shana

I was emailing back and forth a bit with Sharon, telling her how I used the picture of myself with Shauna Lea in all my presentations and what a sweet girl she was, when she told me that Shauna Lea wasn't really her biological daughter, but a child from Planters All Age School who basically asked to come live with her. While telling me how Shauna Lea came to be her daughter, it was here that I learned about Shana-Kay Campbell for the first time and her story.

Sharon wrote to me:

That little girl in the picture is not my biological daughter but she is my daughter. She was a student at Planters, that is where I met her. She hugged me one day and told me she loves me. I took her home for a weekend and she told her mother she wants to live with me. He father was killed by gunmen years ago as a reprisal. She had no birth certificate so I registered her in my name. If I don't tell anyone she is not my biological child, they don't know. She loves me so much. I have another one that I took from state care. She will be 17 on Tuesday. Her father raped her and cut her throat. I give them what I have and do without most times. The seventeen-year-old is in need of constant medical care. She needs a surgery that cannot be done in Jamaica. I had another teenager, but she got pregnant so I had to give her back because I could not manage her and the baby. Her father was killed by the police while he was attacking her. I believe God allows people to reach out to me because of the sacrifices I continue to make for others.

I had known nothing about the seventeen-year-old who lived with Sharon until now. Maybe because we had become close enough friends, she was willing to share the story with me? I asked her more about what happened and why they could not help her in Jamaica.

In layman's terms, they will have to cut both ends of her trachea to get two perfect sections, then build a piece to join both ends in the middle.

It was completely cut off. She has a tube in now. She can't smell. She coughs through it, an opening at her neck. That is where she spits through.

She has to clean it three times per day.

The intestine that carries the feces was also cut in two.

The story made national headlines.

She grew up with her grandmother since she was about two years old. Her father was sent to prison for murder. She was a happy child with her sister and her grandmother. At age fifteen her father was released from prison. She was so happy. However, her happiness was short-lived, as he raped her three months later, in February, while she was home alone. Since then he went in hiding from the police. Children services placed her in the care of an uncle who was instructed not to let her return to the grandparent's house. She went to visit her grandmother one Sunday in September of the same year. While she was there, her father came up behind her from the bushes and pulled her into the bush with a machete at the throat. Her sister and grandmother ran for help. During that time in the bush, he raped her again, cut her tripe, belly and bottom, slit her throat, and stabbed her all over the body. She said he asked her at one point how she was so hard to kill, so she pretended to be dead.

When the police arrived, he was still cutting her, so they shot him in the process. He was pronounced dead on the spot.

She was taken to Annotto Bay Hospital and then air lifted to Cornwall Regional hospital in Montego Bay.

She was in intensive care for months.

During this time, she was placed in state care.

I went to the hospital to visit her and when I saw the condition, my heart bled. Close relatives asked me to take her and promised to help me financially. They ended up leaving it all on me and told me, if I cannot manage, I am to give her back to the government. I could not do that. I applied for legal guardianship and went to court several times and got custody.

Her mother has never been in her life, so it is hard for her. She is an angel. Such a sweet girl.

She has a grand aunt in New York that has been trying to adopt her for more than ten years now. The adoption system in Jamaica is incredibly slow.

She has to take out the tracheal tube each day and clean it several times. She visits the specialist in Montego Bay often for checkups.

But they can't do anything more for her, they just clean it and check for infection. Recently it was infected and she had to have a medicine injected in her throat once per day by a doctor for almost two weeks.

When she spits, it comes up through her throat. It sounds terrible so she is afraid to go out in public. Right now, she has not been to school for over two years.

Reading the short transcript, you are probably feeling what I did when I heard her story for the first time. Shock, anger, sadness, as well as asking God why things like this happen. I hadn't met her before and didn't know anything about her until this moment, but my heart hurt for her. Upon hearing her story, all I wanted to do was reach out to her and hug her and let her know I cared and loved her.

I wrestled with this story in my mind and heart for days. Maybe because it was so horrific, maybe because she was so innocent, or maybe because I just couldn't imagine the reality of it. The fact was that she was in Jamaica and the doctors and hospitals could do nothing further for her.

It bothered me deep inside. She was only seventeen, her whole life ahead of her still. She needed medical attention, surgery that couldn't be performed there in Jamaica, but what about here in America?

I purposely didn't bring up Shana again and instead tried to focus on the wonderful news of the classroom expansion being built. I wanted to enjoy this news and praise God for being allowed to serve Him in such a manner, to help answer the prayers of a community in Old Harbor.

Thoughts of Shana wouldn't go away though; her story had reached my heart. What could I do? I'm not a doctor, I am not even sure what surgery she needs. Who would help her? That question kept nagging at me. Who would help her? This happened two years ago and the doctors in Jamaica can only tell her there is nothing more they can do? Had she lost hope? What must she be thinking? What if that had been me? What could I do? What could I possibly do?

The questions, the thoughts, even the hurt Shana must be feeling penetrated my heart deeper each day after I knew of her story. I wasn't a doctor, but maybe I could at least ask a few physicians for some thoughts. I knew a few that had done visits to various countries in the developing world who might be able to offer some insight. I talked to three whom I knew well, but all the discussions were fruitless. The last one dashed my hopes as he told me he never even heard of a tracheal repair like what she might need. With no medical charts or files and not even knowing Shana personally, I was talking blindly. Again, I tried to convince myself there was nothing I could do for her.

It would have been easy at this point to walk away and know that I at least tried, if only a token amount, but I did try. I let it set in but still I couldn't walk away. Her story haunted me. It hurt me to know how bad she might be suffering in so many ways from all that had happened to her. I prayed to God about her, mostly questioning why and how could this happen to this poor child. What would the rest of her life be like? Not going to school, afraid to go out in public, shots in her neck whenever an infection arose?

After a few more days, I decided maybe I could at least send some letters off to a few doctors and ask for help with this. I wrote letters to about twenty doctors—figuring they will all be too busy to even respond—but I had to try. I dropped names in my letters, told them I was a deacon in the Catholic Church, anything I could think of to get a response from them, hoping to find a sliver of light somewhere.

I must have sent out thirty letters over a few weeks when finally, one Saturday morning, my cell phone rang. It was Dr. Richard Constantino from Rochester General Hospital. He told me that he got my letter and that there was a line in it that prompted his calling:

I know there is little chance of me finding a way, but if God brought her into my life, I must at least try my best. Perhaps God will open a door to me somewhere, but I won't find it unless I try.

He told me he felt the same way, that people come into our lives for a reason. We spoke for a few moments and he agreed to help me. I had never met Dr. Constantino before, but I knew he had some clout at Rochester General Hospital because I had seen his picture on the wall during one of my pastoral visits to the hospital. He went on to tell me that the hospital sometimes donates services for special situations like this, and that he could maybe get the hospital to donate toward helping her. I was thrilled and elated—I had gotten that one "yes" I needed in the midst of all the nay saying I usually get. I was warned not to get too excited because there was much work ahead of us, but we would at least try.

Dr. Constantino with his wife, Jane, gave me the gift of hope that we all need sometimes. I felt renewed and excited, and I was so anxious to tell Sharon. I contacted her right away and told her that I was going to try to help Shana, but that she shouldn't get her hopes up too much. I knew we still had much to overcome. I asked Sharon if we could get Shana's medical charts, as Dr. Constantino needed to see exactly what was going on and what specifically she needed.

Shana's doctor worked at Cornwall Regional Hospital in Montego Bay, the other side of the island and at least a six-hour bus ride for Shana each way every two or three weeks when things were good. If an infection or another issue developed, she had to go more frequently. The doctor had operated on Shana after her attack and saved her life by placing the tracheal tube in her throat. A second operation attempting to improve her situation failed and that was when Shana learned there was nothing more they could do.

I now had someone in the medical field who could help, which was the most important thing to move forward. Dr. Constantino was great at answering my questions. I thought we might bring Shana to Rochester and be able to take care of her, but more difficulties lie ahead. Our first issue was getting Shana's medical records. One thing I have learned about Jamaica is that things tend to move slowly in the country, much slower than I am accustomed to. Sharon called the hospital and was told it would take six to eight weeks to get the medical records. Well, this was not acceptable to me, I wanted them now! (I tend to be rather impatient.) Sharon gave me the phone number to the hospital and Dr. Constantino called but to no avail. The fact that a doctor at the facility would not be the doctor doing the surgery and that he was from another country seemed to be an issue.

I reached out to some friends I had made over the years at the Rochester Jamaican Organization and was put in touch with Dr. Earlando Thomas, who lived in Rochester, but had gone to school at Cornwall Regional Hospital. He had a few connections and was able to help speed up the process to under three weeks.

Once Dr. Constantino had Shana's files and could see the actual needs of Shana, our rollercoaster ride took another turn down as we discovered what Shana needed was beyond Rochester General Hospital's capabilities—in fact, it was beyond the capabilities of almost all hospitals in the United States. My heart sank as Dr. Constantino explained to me how difficult the surgery Shana needed was.

Shana needed a subglottic stenosis surgery. It was a highly specialized surgery that only a small number of doctors could perform. It was so complicated that even most hospitals would not allow it to be performed in their hospitals for fear of litigation or lack of needed services. It seemed like such a big mountain to climb ahead of us. I say the word "us" because Dr. Constantino didn't give up either. It was clear to me that, when I prayed to God for direction and guidance, He sent me Dr. Constantino.

Dr. Constantino reached out to another colleague of his at Rochester General named Dr. Robert Oliver, who is an ENT (ear, nose, and throat) specialist. The two of them went on a search mission across the country looking for a doctor and hospital that would be willing to help. Over the next six weeks, Dr. Constantino would update me with hopeful possibilities in places like New Orleans, Boston, and New York City, but as each hopeful scenario arose, it seemed that within a week or so the hopes were dashed against the rocks.

I would try to relay my hope to Sharon so she could share our updates with Shana, but I was very guarded because I just didn't know what would happen. I could sense Dr. Constantino's doubt sometimes in the tone of his voice, but the man didn't give up. He kept looking for a solution and trying. While I tried not to get my hopes up, it hurt each time to have another scenario fall through. But in my heart, I felt that God had brought us this far and that He would open a door somewhere.

Dr. Constantino was great to me; he would call me back to answer questions and often took the initiative to just call me and update me on how things were going. We had been going back and forth for a couple months when I got the call I was hoping for. It was May 5th, 2015—I'll never forget it. Dr. Constantino had just heard from Dr. Oliver that he had found a doctor and a hospital willing to help. The best part about it was that it was in Cleveland, about a five-hour drive away from me.

The Cleveland Clinic had approved the procedure being done at their facility. Dr. Robert Lorenz, an ENT specialist who had performed similar surgeries, would do the operation.

I was thrilled as Dr. Lorenz's credentials were outstanding. Not only was he a surgeon in the Cleveland Clinic's Head and Neck Institute, but he also was internationally known through his numerous scientific writings and speaking engagements. It was almost too good to be true. I couldn't wait to tell Sharon the news! Dr. Constantino went on, saying that it was going to be an expensive operation so I should brace myself. He estimated $50,000-90,000, but told me that Dr. Lorenz was going to take it to a finance committee meeting and ask for a reduction in fees.

After the meeting, it was determined that the Clinic and Dr. Lorenz would donate 35 percent of the costs to help Shana obtain the surgery she so desperately needed. It was a true blessing not only to find a doctor and a hospital that could do the procedure, but also to find that they were willing to help financially. The final approximated cost for the surgery and other hospital costs would be about $35,000-55,000.

Dr. Oliver later shared this letter with me:

Dr. Oliver,

Dr. Lorenz had requested the below estimate be provided per your inquiry.

Please note that it is not our standard policy to quote prices for services that are not yet scheduled. The following estimated cost is for informational purposes only and in no way obligates the Cleveland Clinic in regards to final charges should you choose to seek treatment here.

The estimated cost for Subglottic Stenosis Surgery is approximately $35,000 to- $55,000.

This estimate is based on other patients who have had similar procedures. This pricing is for self-pay patients.

If you choose to schedule this procedure at Cleveland Clinic, the issue of cost will be revisited and the estimated figures will be reconfirmed with a more precise, formal written estimate.

Please feel free to contact me if you have any further questions or concerns.
Very Respectfully,
Chris

Christopher Sadowski, MD
Manager
Financial Counseling
Global Patient Services, GPS Plus & Transplant
Cleveland Clinic

IN HER OWN WORDS: SHANA'S STORY

Now it was on to the next phase of the journey: trying to raise money. If there is anything I have learned about fundraising over the years, it is that I need help. I always have difficulty asking for help. I believe everyone is already so busy, but the passion in my heart to help someone like Shana always pushes me to ask. Since this project was not going to be ongoing like Eight 4 World Hope, I asked two friends of mine for help: Rod Christian and Tom D'Amico, the current president of Eight 4 World Hope. Both had been to Jamaica with me on separate trips and understood my passion for this mission of serving those in need.

Both said they would help me but we all agreed that we needed to know more about Shana and her story. I reached out to Sharon again, and a few days later, I got a beautiful surprise. The phone rang, and it was Shana herself calling me! She had great difficulty talking, but she just wanted to call me, hear my voice, and say thank you for everything I had done so far. I did most of the talking and Sharon got on the phone to speak for Shana as it was difficult for me to hear her.

I told her how proud I was of her for fighting so courageously and that I would do all I could for her. I also told her that her story touched my heart, and it would be great for her to share it with others who are trying to overcome difficulties in their lives. She agreed and together we decided we should tell her story. What follows is written by Shana-Kay Campbell with the help of her Auntie Sharon.

My name is Shana-Kay Campbell, but most people call me Shana. I must confess that I prefer to be called Shana.

Early Upbringing

I am now 17 years old. I was born on February 10, 1998, in the quiet and cool area of St. Mary known as Guava. You might be wondering if this area is saturated with guavas. This is far from true, but I guess in years gone by that must have been the case.

Guava is actually a district in the community of Lewis Store. The nearest towns to us are Highgate and Annotto Bay. It is a predominantly poor community. The unemployment rate is extremely high and people struggle to provide for their daily needs. It was not uncommon for me to not eat during a day because there was no food.

There are times when we are without water for weeks or even months. Many people depend on agriculture as a means of survival. Such is the situation I was born in. We would walk for miles to the river where we would wash and cook for the day. We would boil the water to drink.

I have five brothers and three sisters. I am the first child for my father and the seventh child for my mother.

My Baby G

I was raised by my grandmother, Mrs. Yvonne Thompson–Campbell, affectionately called Baby G. She is known by many as a hustler. She is hard working and struggles to make ends meet.

Despite the challenges and circumstances, she ensured that my sister and I had a roof over our heads and food on our table most of the time—figuratively speaking, as we had no table. But we were well fed. We had several trees at home from which we could depend on for our meals. We had apples, mangoes, bananas, ackee, coconut, and breadfruit.

She ensured that our basic needs were met.

Baby G would traverse the towns of Annotto Bay, Highgate, and Buff Bay so that we had something to eat. There were times when she went as far as Ocho Rios. Sometimes she hardly had anything in her bags to sell but she was committed to taking care of us.

My biological mother

My biological mother is Carol Livingston. She has her own story and struggles in life. By the time Sabrina and I entered the world, our brothers and sisters were big men and women. Even though we lived with our grandmother, my mother would visit us often, whenever she found it possible. I know she loves us, but she isn't able to help care for us. She has six other children apart from my sister Sabrina and me. She left us when I was two years old; I think my father used to beat her really badly so she thought it was best for her to leave us with my grandparents. She lives in Spanish Town now but she moves around quite often. I know she has battled addiction and mental health issues throughout her life but she is still my mother and I will always love her.

Sabrina, my baby sister

I call her Sub. People say we are different but I believe we are alike in so many ways, even though she is a little bit bossy. She acts as if she is the bigger one at times.

I would not trade her for anyone else, she is my baby sister. Sabrina and I have been through so much together. We've laughed and cried together. We planned for the future, what we would become, and how we would look after the needs of our grandmother.

I am more trusting than she is. It takes a lot for her to trust someone. It was evident that she did not like our father. Sabrina would communicate her feelings towards him when we sit for girls' chat. She was of the view that he looks evil. I remember her saying, "I do not like the look on his face. He looks guilty."

She did not hide her feelings regarding him. That is Sub. She tells you her mind. No matter what the result.

She told him blatantly that she does not like him. She would eye him, not trusting him.

Sabrina was the outgoing type. She loves to go out with friends and have a good time. I think this was her way of escaping what was happening around her.

Cousin Marian

I could not write without telling you something about cousin Marian. Some call her Wingie—trust me, she is not small at all. I lived with her for about two years after which I returned to my grandmother. I was about four at the time.

I remember her bathing me, washing my hair, and putting me to bed—just being nice to me. I was so sad when she had to leave me behind. She migrated from St. Mary to Kingston. But those days were fun. She loved and cared for me.

My father – before prison

My father was incarcerated in Kingston. At that time, I was about one year and eight months old. What can I remember? Nothing, to be honest. I can only recall what has been said to me.

I was told he committed murder and was sentenced to life imprisonment. My grandmother told us he would serve approximately twelve-and-a-half years in prison after which he could be considered for parole. He was released in December 2012.

My father – in prison

While he was incarcerated, he would send ice-cream money for us when my grandmother visited him. I remember receiving calls from him and he would inquire how we were doing.

I recall once he asked us to sing for him. Funny as it may sound, we loved our father and anticipated the time when he would come home.

He promised to look after us and that things would be different. It was really a difficult task for Grandma Baby G to care for us and our father in prison. She would sell articles of clothing and fish at the market and used her last dollar to send us to school and visit him in prison.

I can vividly recall the bags of items she had to pack for him, especially the fried fish.

My grandmother sold anything she could catch her hands on. She is a resilient woman.

Prison visits

My father was placed at General Penitentiary, dubbed GP. Family Day is a special activity undertaken by the institution. This is a time when children can visit and spend time with their fathers while they are imprisoned. Hold them. Touch them. Hug them. Just be with them.

While the time was short, we looked forward to this time each year. Sabrina and I would journey with our Grandmother in the early hours of the morning to Kingston. We tried to arrive early each time to get an early number. They used a ticket system.

We would take pictures, talk and look forward to the future. In spite of what he did and why he was in prison, my thoughts reflected on the fact that he was my father. And even if it was just for this moment, that was all that mattered to me.

So, prison visits became a part of our family traditions. I must tell you this, the scariest part of the experience was when the big gate closed behind us. I wondered: What if we were locked in and unable to get out? Just a thought.

His release

I remember that people visited us from the probation department in 2012. They asked us how we felt about our father's impending release. They also questioned us about how we would adjust to the new experience. After all, I had few memories of him except for the times we visited him on special occasions in prison.

I'll return to this point.

We knew he was coming home and we were happy. We weren't sure what to expect, but we were happy.

We all know that every little girl wants her father's love. I have never ever experienced that in my life.

So the thought of my father coming home excited me. I thought my protector was coming. I thought he would be my provider. I thought he would work and assist my grandmother who has been playing his role for over fourteen years.

I thought our life would somehow be different but in a positive way.

I remembered the night he came home. Yes, the night!

I did not know he was coming at that moment so when I saw him exiting the car, I was shocked. I was shocked but excited. Sabrina and I ran to him. We hugged him.

Unfortunately, our happiness was short-lived.

The day my life changed

Soon after the release of my father from prison, I became ill. I had a bad cold that prevented me from attending school. Being that my grandmother had to work to provide for the family, she asked my father to take me to the doctor. After all, he was my father.

When I came back home from seeing the doctor, I was tired so I changed my clothes and decided to lie down in my room. My father was on the couch watching television. I picked up that he was looking at me in a suspicious manner. However, I shrugged off the feeling. After all, he is my father. The one I have waited for to come home.

Somehow, I got scared.

I got scared because I had had a previous altercation with him. One night after he came home from prison, I was watching television in bed and got up to go for a sheet. He came in the room and lay down beside me on the bed.

I did not think much of it, as he was my father. He proceeded to move over me. He held me down and covered my mouth with his hand. He lay on top of me. I pushed him away, got up, and ran to my grandparents' room.

I was breathless and could not speak. My grandfather asked me repeatedly what the matter was. Finally, I was able to regain my composure and told them that my father had tried to rape me.

My grandfather was mad and ran him out of the house, but he came back. Grandpa worked in Kingston and was often gone. When he wasn't there, Grandma let my father come back, she just didn't say anything. My father apologized over and over and even gave me money and begged me to forgive him but I was still really afraid of him.

It was the end of May and I didn't feel good so I missed school and went to the hospital. On this particular day after returning from the doctor, I felt scared.

He laid on the bed beside me and asked, "Are you afraid of me?"

I told him yes. He told me not to be afraid of him.

In Jamaican Patois, he said, "nuh fraid a mi."

He proceeded to push me onto the bed. He then ripped off my underwear. I was so scared. I screamed and begged him not to hurt me.

I started to fight him and he told me to open my legs. He kept repeating the command to open my legs. I pressed my legs together as hard as I could.

I looked at the table beside the bed and realized that a pair of scissors was close to me. I reached for it and tried to stab him in his back. That was the only escape I could think of. He saw the pair of scissors in my hand and he bit my hand so hard. I had to let go of the scissors.

The mark from that bite is still visible on my right hand.

I saw a strange look in his eyes. I asked him, "Are you going to kill me?"

"Yes," he replied.

I started to negotiate with him. I begged him: "Please let me go, please let me go. I promise if you let me go, I will not tell anyone."

I told him it would just be between the two of us.

He told me no. According to him, if he allowed me to go, I would report on him. I tried to convince him I would not.

When he was about to enter, I screamed that I was a virgin. I do not know what happened but he let me go.

I jumped through the window and ran next door. I told the neighbors, and the police got involved. The matter was also reported to the Child Development Agency.

He stabbed my cousin, who was passing the house, when I ran. She was stabbed in the belly and had to be admitted to the hospital. I guess he thought she saw or heard something. After that incident, he went into hiding.

I did not return to school after the incident because I was so ashamed of myself, of what happened to me. So I stayed home for the remainder of the school term and during the summer holidays. During this time, I asked to be transferred to a new school. I felt a different environment would be good for me because everybody still knew what had happened to me.

Summer was finally coming to an end. I got registered at a new school and was expected to start on Monday, September 9, 2013.

But everything changed the day before. It had been about five months since my father had attacked me. I heard he had been watching me but I had started to not give it as much thought. That Sunday I was home with my grandmother and my sister Sabrina. We were preparing roasted breadfruit, ackee, and salt fish for breakfast. It was a regular Sunday morning.

My father ran into the yard. Sabrina was on the phone.

Sabrina later told me that he came into the house and held a machete around her neck. He had never hurt her before, and she later told me that she was not afraid of him.

My little cousin came inside the house and saw what was happening. She said that she saw my father with the machete at Sabrina's neck. She ran outside and screamed for help.

He realized what was happening so he released Sabrina and

she ran away. After she ran, he went into the room where I was cooking and held on to me from behind. I was roasting breadfruit with Baby G.

He placed the machete to my neck and pulled me with him to the bushes. My grandmother and my sister screamed. They begged. They cried. They called for help.

In the bushes

While in the bushes I asked him, "Why? Why are you doing this to me?"

He said I told everyone what he did, forcing him to live in the bushes like a criminal or a dog.

He asked me if I remembered the day he told me that he was going to kill me.

"You think I was joking?" he asked. "Well, I am going to kill you today."

I started to beg for my life. "Please do not kill me. I am only 15. I don't want to die," I pleaded.

I was so shocked. I could not believe what was happening to me. I thought it was a nightmare.

I tried to cry but no tears came.

All this time I was praying, "Lord, I don't want to die. I don't want to die. Please."

He had a knife and he used it to cut off my underwear. He started to fondle me with his fingers. I heard him say that his penis was not coming up. He started to masturbate.

He then stabbed me in the neck at the front. That was the beginning of many cuts. He told me that he rubbed garlic on the knife because it would ease the hurt of being stabbed. I did not really feel when the knife cut into my skin. It felt numbed. I saw blood shooting from my neck. I realized then that I was badly wounded.

I was there talking to him, still trying to think of something that would cause him to let me go—talking, hoping he would be convinced to let me go. I had to hold my throat to talk as my voice was starting to go away.

I even asked him, "Why you had to take me? Why you didn't take my sister?"

He just would not listen. He refused to budge. He asked me why I had done this to him, I was his favorite. He told me I was making him do this to me. All I could do was wonder how this could be all my fault.

Then he stabbed me in the belly. I could see my intestines protruding. Later on, at the hospital I had to wear a colostomy bag as a result of this wound.

I laid there bleeding for what seemed thirty minutes. He told me that he would have to stab me again. In fact, he told me that I was taking too long to die. In Jamaican Patois, "Yuh a tek too long fi dead."

I tried to think of things to say so that he would let me go. I wondered where everyone was, why nobody was helping me. He then asked me where else he should stab me.

"Please don't stab me anymore," I begged. All my pleas fell on deaf ears.

He asked me where he should stab me again, so I told him to stab me in my side. I hurt so badly and didn't know what to say.

I pretended to be dead and laid there for a long time. He thought I was dead. Because I was bleeding from my neck and it was badly wounded, I could not hold my breath for too long.

I started to breathe out loudly, making him realize I was not dead. This made him upset.

He told me that he would stab me again because the police officers would arrive soon. He told me that the police officers were going to kill him and that both of us have to die together. He said that he was prepared to die because he was not returning to prison.

It was then that he stabbed me one more time at a different place in my abdomen.

"Please bring me to the hospital. I don't want to die," I pleaded with him.

I don't know where I got the energy, but I got up and ran. All I was thinking was: I do not want to die. I am too young to die.

I got up and started to run. I was impeded by the bushes, preventing me from moving faster.

He came after me and held on to me. He was so mad. He then stabbed me in the back of my neck.

About thirty minutes after that, he said to me, "You nah dead?"

He raised the machete as if to cut off my head.

Suddenly, some men from the community came into the bushes and started to throw big stones at him.

He shouted to them, "Mine unu lick mi baby!"

Translation: "Be careful, you'll hit my baby."

The police then came and told him to hold up his hands. I am not sure what happened next, but I heard shots being fired. He fell beside me and I saw blood flowing from his nose.

I was not sure whether he was dead. Men came with sticks and machetes and beat him. I was too weak to move. I had lost so much blood.

It was then that I heard someone saying, "The girl is not dead, she is not dead."

I felt someone lift me and run with me to a vehicle that took me to the hospital.

I was then unconscious.

I only remember waking up in Cornwall Regional Hospital in Montego Bay.

I was later told that I was taken to the Annotto Bay Hospital in St. Mary—where they did an emergency surgery to stop the bleeding—after which I was airlifted to Cornwall Regional Hospital.

Hospital stay

I must confess that I absolutely hate hospitals. On the other hand, I have to say, I had the best experience at this hospital. Dr. Davis, took special care of me. The intensive team was the best. They ensured that I was well attended to and separated from persons who just wanted to see the girl who was on the TV news.

My grandmother and family members visited me. My biological mother stayed by my side. She even slept on the bench at the hospital. The nurses made sure that I was well catered to.

How our lives changed

During this time my sister Sabrina became a ward of the state and was placed in state care. That made her so sad and bitter. She felt that she was only forced into the state's care because of what happened to me. She questioned why she was taken even though nothing happened to her.

My cousin, whom we both called Auntie Sharon, came to her aid. She travelled to St. Mary and applied to the courts and Child Development Agency to have Sabrina placed in her care. The case was transferred to Spanish Town, and after several court appearances, Sabrina was placed in the care of Auntie Sharon and her husband, Uncle Kevin.

After spending almost four months at the hospital, I was wondering where the government was going to send me. After being released from the hospital, I spent some time at Blossom Gardens Children's Home. I must say thanks to the manager, Mrs. Brown, for being there for me.

I grew homesick and I wondered what would happen to me. I was not sure if Auntie Sharon would take both of us. I prayed, and God answered my prayers. Auntie Sharon told the court that she would also take me in when I was released from the hospital, and it was granted. She became my legal guardian, and I was given a new title of "foster kid."

Auntie Sharon had to explain everything to us numerous times. Things were challenging for us, but we were well cared for. We were never hungry. Auntie always said, if there is only one banana, we'll share it.

I became an outpatient at Cornwall Regional Hospital. This meant that I had to find the means to travel to Montego Bay regularly for checkups. This was a costly venture but I always kept my appointments. Each appointment cost $8,000 Jamaican dollars, about $75 in U.S. dollars, and I had to go one or two times each month.

My aunt would contact CDA each time and arrangements were made for me to sleep at Blossom Gardens, sometimes for the week, to be able to access treatment at the hospital.

Surgery

Eventually, it reached a point where the doctors in Jamaica were unable to do anything else for me. Dr. Davis tried his best to get other doctors to consent to the surgery but he faced several road blocks. However, he never gave up. God bless this man.

I remembered my Auntie praying for me one day. It was not an ordinary prayer. She told me she felt that this was it that God would work something out for me. This encouraged me to have faith and believe.

One day she said that she told a white man about me. I later learned that his name was Kevin Carges, one of the founders of Eight 4 World Hope, a U.S.-based nonprofit organization. Kevin was moved by my story and all that I had been through. He told my aunt that he was not promising anything but he was going to make some contacts. The rest is history.

He encouraged me to share my story. He told me to write down my thoughts, - everything. I started doing that and I found hope and strength in the process.

I told my aunt that I was shy, and she promised to be with me all the way. Auntie Sharon told me that I had a powerful story and a life-changing testimony. She reminded me that good things can come out of a negative situation.

My little neighbor Aja Allen heard my Aunt talking to me, and she said, "Shana, just speak from your heart." Aja was just eight years old at the time and God used her to tell me that.

On May 22nd, 2015, I spoke on the phone with Kevin for the first time. He brought new hope to my life.

I kept thinking to myself, how can a person I do not even know love me so much? How can he be doing so much for me? I was further moved when he said, "You are my family."

Struggling to Fulfill Our Dream

On June 24th, 2015, Shana and I finally got a chance to meet in person and spend some time together. It was a great day for me. My daughter, Katy, and I flew down to Jamaica for the dedication of the new school expansion project at Davis Primary School.

I was so happy to be there. I felt incredibly blessed to see the new building open, as well as see Sharon, Shauna Lea, and my other 737 children at the school. I also finally had a chance to meet Shana for the first time and share the whole experience Katy during her first time there.

Once I arrived at the school, I started getting hugs from the children. Anyone who knows me knows how much I love hugs. I must have hugged at least 300 children that day.

I could write a whole book just about Davis Primary and Eight 4 World Hope, but I'll stay focused on what (or rather, who) this book is about: Shana. After the ceremony and subsequent party to celebrate, I walked outside and saw her sitting down with Sharon's mother-in-law, Garnet. The first thing I noticed was her beautiful smile. I walked over and introduced myself. It was great to finally meet her.

It was hard to understand and hear her at times as she could not talk very loudly or without difficulty, but we managed. After the dedication Shana (along with Shauna Lea and another of Sharon's daughters, Gracie) joined me to finish up some other work I had to do before we went back to our hotel to relax and have dinner.

I sat between Sharon and Shana that evening during dinner and learned much more about her and her situation. She reminded me of my own daughter, Katy, who happened to be the same age of 17. Shana is your typical teenage girl in most regards. She loves shopping and texting on the phone. I know that by the time I left Jamaica, I felt like I had another daughter, and I was determined to do all I could to help her get the best care available.

Now that I had met Shana and felt like I knew her better, I got together with my friends, Rod and Tom, and we started to formulate a fundraising plan for the surgery and subsequent costs associated with bringing her and Sharon here to America for the surgery.

After a while Shana began to know me better and trust me more. She shared a couple journal entries with me that she wrote after her attack before I met her. These two entries will give you a glimpse into her mental state by the time I met her.

September 2014

Sometimes I wish I was born into another family so I wouldn't have to go through all I've gone through now. I wish I wasn't so ignorant and poor, broken and angry. I wish my mind wasn't so dark and full of hate. I mean is it normal for someone to hate themselves this much? My reflection irritates me. I feel like I could just crawl out of my body. I feel like I'm living but dead.

November 2014

I want to disappear, I want to go somewhere nobody knows me. I want to start over with new people. I don't know them, they don't know me. Run away so people think I am dead and will be forgotten—out of sight, out of mind, they say. They'll forget about me easily; besides I didn't play an important part of their lives, I can easily be replaced. There is nothing special about me. I'm not special, just different, just very different. I'm an embarrassment and a disappointment I'm told but it's okay, I didn't expect nothing better from myself. I guess I'm destined to be a failure in life. I can either do something and not care what people say and live my life the way I want, or agree with what they say and be sad and miserable the rest of my life.

Shana's story was so compelling to me that I thought it would be fairly easy to raise the money. It was agreed that we would need close to $60,000 for the throat surgery and the plastic surgery to repair the scarring all over her torso and neck. Other expenses would include medicines, counseling, and various therapies such as speech, plus basics like travel, food, and clothing.

Shana was a ward of the state of Jamaica given that she was essentially an orphan after her father was killed by the police during his attack on her. The Child Development Agency was responsible for Shana, and, that being the case, they should support her financially for the cost of the surgery.

I was put in contact with Ms. Audrey Budhi who would help raise the needed funds for Shana's surgery. Since the surgery was not possible in Jamaica, they had pretty much written Shana off as there was nothing more they could do. Once I had secured a hospital and a doctor who would do the surgery, the CDA would have to start coming up with the money somehow.

The country of Jamaica is in bad shape, and I was told right from the start that they could not promise me the funds could be secured for the surgery. Still, I figured I would put in a proposal for the full amount needed ($60,000) in the hopes I might get some of it, if not all.

In case the country could not fund the surgery fully, we decided we should set out to raise the funds ourselves. I hoped that the CDA would come up with some, and we could raise the rest.

Rod created a GoFundMe type page, and we launched it thinking we would have great success if we could just share Shana's story. We started to promote it on Facebook and other social media outlets in the hope that it would go viral, and after two weeks, we had only raised $950. I was discouraged to say the least.

Shana's Surgery
Organized by: Rod Christian

The Story:

Shana was 15 when her father attacked her on a Sunday morning in the family's yard. He stabbed and slashed her repeatedly with a machete, telling her that she was taking too long to die. Shana pretended to be dead before finally losing consciousness and waking up in the hospital in Montego Bay, Jamaica. A year earlier, "the thought of my father coming home from jail excited me. I thought my protector was coming. I remember the night he came home. I was so excited. Unfortunately, my happiness was short-lived."

Two years later, Shana bears scars all over her body. She no longer attends school and admits that she is very self-conscious. She has had two tracheotomies, one to save her life and another that left her with complex respiratory issues. Her doctor in Jamaica says they can do no more and that what she needs is beyond the hospital's ability. Shana requires a "sub-carina tracheal repair" that will enable her to breathe, speak and eat with less difficulty, reduce the risk of infection, and prolong her life.

Kevin Carges, the founder of Eight 4 World Hope, a non-profit agency in Rochester, New York that raises funds for special projects in developing countries, learned of Shana's plight in January through her guardian and aunt, Sharon Campbell-Danvers, a school principal in Jamaica. Kevin then got in touch with Dr. Richard Constantino and Dr. Robert Oliver of Rochester General Hospital, who have arranged for Shana's complex surgery at the Cleveland Clinic later this year. The Clinic is donating much of the operation's true cost. A highly-specialized surgical team will heal the hole in Shana's throat, but it is the kindness of strangers that will help heal the hole in Shana's heart.

"I spoke with Kevin for the first time on May 22nd," writes Shana. "He has brought new hope to my life. I kept thinking to myself, "How can a person I do not even know love me so much? How can he be doing so much for me? I was so moved when he told me, 'You are my family.' I see God in action."

Donations totaling $60,000 are needed for a pre-surgical

visit and assessment this summer, transportation, surgery, continued counseling and related expenses for Shana.

While Shana's story had touched my heart, it was perhaps just another story in a world full of difficulties and hurts. I also had to realize that, through my group, I had spent the last five years begging my friends and family to help me build schools in Jamaica. All my efforts had been to help 1,700 children each school year, but this was just one person.

My next step was to start reaching out to larger media outlets such as newspapers and TV stations. I began to write letters to people who could help me (the TV stations, and all the local newspapers) thinking if, I could just get Shana's story out, people would respond to help her.

Each day I would find a columnist in a newspaper and send them an email sharing the story, and each day I would get no response. I sent emails to all the TV stations, even one that interviewed me once about my group, and I never heard back.

Quite honestly, it hurt. Shana's story had touched my heart and, after meeting her and seeing her smile first-hand, I was committed to helping her, but I was failing.

Perhaps it was God's way of telling me that I was overconfident, a reminder that God's work isn't easy, or that the devil was always there ready to build on my feelings of discouragement.

After a solid month of reaching out to anyone who would listen, I had raised about $3,000. I reached out to Rod and Tom again searching for ideas. I wasn't ready for such a difficult time raising the money.

Rod had the idea of sending personal letters to people we knew, sharing Shana's story and making a personal plea for help. We each made a list and sent off letters in the hopes that our friends would respond. We sent out 50 letters in total and got responses from at least half of them. It was a big boost to me as it put us over the $10,000 mark and it felt like we were making progress at last. I also held out hope that the CDA would come through with money to help support Shana.

I started to reach out to my home parish of Our Lady of Peace in Geneva, New York, through an article in the parish bulletin. I was also finally able to get an article published in the Finger Lakes Times through my friend, Mike Cutillo. Money drifted in and, as a few months passed, the amount collected was closer to $15,000.

I began to work with Sharon as a way of reaching out to the people of Jamaica. After a few calls, she was able to get an article written about Shana that would appear in the national newspaper of Jamaica, the Observer. After all, when Shana was attacked, it was a national story, so a follow-up piece seemed in order. The article ran in November 2015 and generated over sixty comments from readers, but little money. This wasn't surprising, since many in Jamaica lack the resources to help others in need, but a few thousand dollars were raised and we kept inching towards our goal.

Shana Kay Campbell reflects as she prepares to speak with the Sunday Observer. (PHOTOS: NAPHTALI JUNIOR)

Shana Kay Campbell focused on leading a normal life.
Teen who was attacked by dad in St Mary fights on.

By Penda Honeyghan
Sunday Observer writer
Sunday, November 22, 2015

SHANA Kay Campbell was not prepared for the events that would unfold on the morning of September 8, 2013 as she made breakfast with her grandmother in the usually quiet community of Guava, Lewistore, St Mary.

The usually serene Sunday morning quickly transformed into a bloody scene of crime following a near-death attack on then 15-year-old Campbell, who was kidnapped, chopped and stabbed several times over the body by her father, Wayne Campbell, who had months before been released from prison.

Today, two years after the attack, her legal guardian and cousin, Sharon Campbell-Danvers, is appealing for assistance so that Campbell can undergo a life-enhancing surgery. The sub-carina tracheal repair operation would allow the now 17-year-old to breathe, speak and eat with less difficulty, in addition to reducing the risks of her contracting infection while prolonging her life.

"I have been exploring my options for years trying to give

Shana a normal chance of life, because what is happening to her is not fair. But the doctors here have done all that they could. Following the incident, Shana had two tracheotomies, one to save her life and another that left her with complex respiratory issues. She said the doctors in Jamaica say that they can do no more and what she needs is beyond the hospital's capabilities," Campbell-Danvers explained.

Having learned this, Campbell-Danvers sought international support, which saw her connecting with Kevin Carges, founder of Eight 4 Hope World, a non-profit organization in Rochester, New York, that raises funds for special projects in developing countries, with whom she shared Campbell's plight.

"Kevin was very touched when he was made aware of Shana's ordeal and immediately made contact with Dr Richard Constantino and Dr Robert Oliver of Rochester General Hospital, who have arranged for Shana's complex surgery at the Cleveland Clinic later this year. The doctors are now preparing paperwork for her December 7 embassy interview date," Campbell-Danvers stated.

But, even as Campbell's chance of normal life is closer to realisation, her guardian, who is also a school principal, has hit yet another major hurdle. She is unable to find the additional money that is required for her to perform the highly specialised surgery.

"The clinic is donating much of the operation's true cost. A highly-specialised surgical team will heal the hole in Shana's throat, but it is the kindness of strangers that will help heal the hole in Shana's heart," Campbell-Danvers pleaded.

She said donations totalling US$60,000 which, when broken down, in Jamaican dollars amount to just over $7 million, is needed for a pre-surgical visit and assessment, transportation, surgery, continued counselling and related expenses. She has since opened a ScotiaBank account at the Old Harbour branch and persons wishing to assist Campbell can make contributions to 408629. She said that she may also be contacted at 353-4901.

She described it as a heartbreaking experience, not only for her and Campbell's biological mother and grandmother who are very supportive but are unable to contribute much because of their employment status, but for Campbell as well who has become over-excited by the prospects of her quality of life improving.

"I know that it is a lot to ask, but I sit home every day trying to keep sane, writing my poetry or fixing and cleaning everything that has already been fixed and cleaned dozens of times, just wishing that it was all a dream. I want to go to school, to walk freely without puzzling eyes staring me down wanting answers for the reason there is a band attached to my neck or why there is a hole in my throat," a tearful Campbell vented.

"I just hope that someone out there can help me. I try not to be so self-conscious or ashamed to walk on the street, but how can I not when the last time I was encouraged to go out my spit fell close to someone because I don't always have control of what exits in the trachea," she pleaded.

"Was it wrong of me to be excited about my father's release from jail?" Campbell asked, as she paused still after two years trying to fathom the reason behind his gruesome attack and desire to leave her lifeless.

Campbell's father had been imprisoned for 13 years on a murder charge, and even as she tried to understand him and appreciate his return to her life, he attempted to rape her after she return early from school while not feeling so well. Having reported the incident, Campbell's father fled, evading the police over several weeks and camping out in bushes. But it was not long before he returned, this time with the intention to exact fatal revenge.

"I was home with my grandmother and sister cooking breakfast with my grandmother, he came up with a machete and grabbed me from behind, pulled me into the bushes, and he said that I was the reason he was a fugitive. He then stabbed me in the neck, then the stomach, he cut my underwear before stabbing me in the stomach. He said I was taking too long to die, before asking where next I wanted him to stab or chop me before *stabbing me in the side. I pleaded with him not to kill me, but he said I had to die," Campbell said reflecting on horrors of the morning of September 8, 2013.*

She said that luckily for her, her grandmother and sister saw what was happening, but her machete-wielding father prevented anyone from coming close to her as she was by then unconscious. It was not until the police came, strategised and shot her father who had been clinging to her body, that they were able to rescue her.

She admitted that she sometimes is unable to live but joined her foster mother, her biological mother and grandmother in thanking the officers of the Child Development Agency (CDA) and the nurses at the Cornwall Regional Hospital and the Annotto Bay Hospital for always being supportive of her, noting that even as they have tried to source funding for the operation, the CDA too has made several attempts, all of which have been futile.

"If only people knew what she has been through, many people thinking she died. Months in the hospital, copious amounts of treatment after surgery, and being unable to smell or taste... having to remove and clean three to four times daily, a tube that controls your breathing, or being completely unaware of the foul stench it lets off when it becomes infected, or having to wear a colostomy bag for months, or having to hold your hand to a trachea every time she needs to speak. That is real pain, but it is also strength. I hope that the people of Jamaica can help Shana to regain the life that was stolen from her. Please help us," a tearful Campbell-Danvers pleaded.

It was a wonderful article, but it was still discouraging to have raised less than half of what we needed after six months of trying. All I could do was accept that this would happen for Shana on God's time, not mine. While I continued to pray for Shana's health, I started to ask God for patience and understanding for the difficulty I was having getting the funds I needed. I prayed for God to show me a way, to open a door to me that would help. I was losing hope in getting anything from the CDA.

Shana was also feeling the discouragement. Sharon told me that she was feeling sullen and down. I think she had placed her hopes in the CDA, yet after six months, there was nothing.

The only good news we received during the last month was that Shana had gotten her visa and passport. After talking with my wife Jackie, we decided to invite Shana to America to join our family for Christmas. It would be her first time to America, and I have to admit it saddened me when I asked her what she wanted for Christmas and her response was, "What do you mean? Like a present? I don't know, I've never gotten a Christmas present before."

FROM JAMAICA TO THE U.S.

It was Shana's first time flying, flying alone to a place she had never been to stay with a family she hardly knew—all when she was only seventeen years old. I can only imagine the courage or perhaps the desperation to have the surgery going through her mind as she headed out. I had a friend of mine, Deacon Fred Toca, help her through the connecting flight in Atlanta. God is always watching out for Shana, it seems. What are the chances I have a friend who is a deacon assigned to the airport in Atlanta through which Shana happens to be making a connecting flight? I would have had no idea that he was even there had I not spoken to him by chance at a gathering for Catholic Relief Services in Baltimore a few months earlier.

I had been so worried about her finding her way through that large airport, but there was God, working through Deacon Fred, helping her along. Fred was there to guide her from customs to her connecting flight to Rochester, and even bought her a slice of pizza along the way. She got on her connecting flight just fine and my daughter, Allison, and I met her in Rochester. It was so great to see Shana finally come down the pathway as she just followed everyone else. not really knowing where to go.

When we finally gave her a welcoming hug, she was shivering quite a bit, so I gave her my coat and Allison gave her a scarf and we proceeded to the luggage carousel to get her suitcase.

It was hard to believe Shana was even here. I had known nothing about her ten months ago and now she was here to stay with my family for three weeks. I marveled at how much God had done in such a short time, and I felt blessed that I could be a small part in His plan for her.

After we got her suitcase, we headed for the Rochester bench at the airport to take a picture and let her Aunt Sharon know that she had arrived safe and sound. The whole thing really hit me in the airport: how she had survived the brutal attack to begin with, how she was staying with her cousin Sharon with little to no hope of ever having the surgery she needed, and how I had no idea she even existed ten months ago. Yet here she was, a new member of our family. I was looking forward to knowing her better and showing her a bit of America as well as visiting several doctors to see if helping her was even possible.

As we drove home, I think the thing that surprised Shana the most was how clean and open things were. Open as in not being fenced-in; crime is so rampant in Jamaica that every business and home has a fence around it.

We stopped by Dunkin Donuts to pick up my daughter-Katy, from work. Katy brought Shana a hot chocolate with whipped cream, a whole new experience in itself to warm her up a bit. We continued on to our house as she saw homes decorated with Christmas lights, snowflakes drifting through the air, and the beauty of America for the very first time.

As we pulled into our driveway, Shana remarked how she couldn't believe that the houses didn't have fences around them, and that everything was so open. We walked into the house where she met my wife, Jackie, for the first time. As they hugged each other, our dog, Finn, ran into the living room excited to see our new guest. Poor Shana, having never seen a pet before and only knowing wild dogs in Jamaica, immediately jumped onto the couch and hid behind Jackie. We all laughed. Finn is a very gentle dog who is practically afraid of his own shadow. We had to realize that everything here was going to be very different and new to Shana, and we just couldn't assume anything. Anticipating Shana's visit, I had reached out to every TV anchor and reporter, local newspaper columnist, and radio program host to see if they could help me share Shana's story. I literally reached out to more than two dozen people seeking help, and only one responded: Jennifer Burke from the Catholic Courier.

We were at Shana's first doctor appointment at the University of Rochester Strong Memorial Hospital meeting with an internal medicine doctor when Jennifer called me requesting an interview. Shana had complained of pain in her stomach, but the hospital staff determined that she was okay, and that the pains were from scar tissue in her intestine area from the attacks and subsequent surgeries.

After receiving the good news, we drove to the Catholic Courier to meet Jennifer. I had the previous article about her written in the Jamaican Observer that told much of her story, and I went on to tell Jennifer the rest of the story of our hopes and how our partnership developed. She wanted a picture to include for the newspaper story, so she asked Shana what she wanted to see and do while in the United States. She was shy and said very little during the interview, but she did say that she wanted to see the zoo. We set up a meeting with the staff photographer at the Seneca Park Zoo to take pictures. It was a really cold day, but we still managed to have some fun - and, most importantly, I had found my first outlet in the media to share Shana's story.

Later in the week, we went to visit Dr. Constantino, so he could meet Shana and administer a general exam. Her doctor visits in Jamaica were generally to the emergency room for tracheal tube treatments. The exam went well and she was in good shape.

We immediately went over to see Dr. Oliver, the ENT specialist. He did an exam of her throat firsthand to see the damage from the attack. He was encouraged by the results and he felt that Dr. Lorenz should be able to help her. He was very positive and reaffirming to Shana and she left his office feeling great that her prayers might actually get answered. She was so happy; I'll never forget the joy she exuded on the way home that day.

Of course, we still had to meet Dr. Lorenz. He would be the deciding factor in all of this because he would be the one actually doing the surgery. I had been talking back and forth with his assistant, Traci Kishmarton, who was so kind and supportive and made everything less stressful, as I coordinated everything for the trip to Cleveland and the Clinic.

It was almost five hours of driving before we reached the Clinic. It is a beautiful hospital, and everyone I met there was wonderful. I was truly impressed with the facility as well as the staff in all regards.

When we met with Dr. Lorenz, he was very kind and comforting to Shana. I really appreciated that, as I had become quite fond and protective of her during her visit with us. He placed the scope down her throat and did an exam to see if the surgery would be viable for her. The news was bittersweet, and I could see the look of dejection on Shana's face as he shared his thoughts.

Her throat was more damaged than was previously realized. He said he could fix the hole in her throat, but she would never regain her voice; or he could give her back a strong voice, but the hole and tracheal tube would have to remain in for the rest of her life.

Shana would have to make a choice, but she would never fully regain what was taken from her. We drove about an hour in silence back home as the reality set in. At seventeen years old, it must be hard to accept certain things—even at fifty it would be hard—but I could not imagine being so young and having something like this happen.

After about an hour, Shana spoke up and said, "This is silly, of course I'm going to have the hole repaired."

I looked at her and said, "That's what I would do. People will no longer stare at you, and you have the choice of talking to those you want to. No more emergency room visits because of an infection in your throat, no more sitting around hospitals for days waiting for help or for them to find the proper tubing. I would fully support whatever you choose, but I think you are making the right choice."

Shana smiled and seemed to instantly regain her happy and joyful self again. I felt good about the visit and the fact that we could help her, and thought to myself that maybe Dr. Lorenz was hedging his words so as not to get her hopes up too high.

We tried to make the rest of Shana's stay as fun as possible while we celebrated the Christmas season. We did all sorts of yuletide activities, including attending an Amerks hockey game, A Christmas Carol at Geva Theatre, and Disney on Ice. She also tried new and different foods as well as attending church with me at my parish community of Our Lady of Peace in Geneva, New York, and in her faith belief at Bay Knoll Seventh Day Adventist in Irondequoit, New York, where we both found much support.

Shana went back home in mid-January, having seen America for the first time. She had lots of fun, and we accomplished a great deal with doctor appointments and some future press in the Catholic Courier newspaper. It was also good for me since we had a lot of time to talk and get to know each other much better. We had some deep talks during the car rides, in the waiting rooms, and just while trying out some new foods at various restaurants. I came to understand her feelings and what she had been dealing with over these last few years.

What a brave young lady Shana is. But the difficult part of it for me was her not being able to see the good in herself. As she looked for understanding, she perhaps forgot or couldn't see the good in her, the beautiful heart that is shy, but loves easily and tries to find the good in every situation. Shana must have said at least five times that others suffer more than she does and that she is grateful for what she has. She felt blessed and loved by God, but the other side still lurked within her.

We all search for answers, why things are the way they are—the meaning behind things. During this time, Shana struggled to understand why this happened to her, thinking she did something wrong and deserved it. She asked herself, does God not love me? Sometimes I wish

I had all the answers but all I could do was tell her how much I loved her and that God loved her so much that no human could fully understand or express it properly.

I got an email from Jennifer Burke at the Catholic Courier about a week after Shana returned home. We clarified a few things about what the doctor visits entailed, and I updated her on Shana. The first week in February, the article she wrote came out. I was thrilled!

Deacon Raises Funds for Teen's Surgery

Courier photos by Jeff Witherow
Shana Campbell, 17, exhales to see her breath during a visit to Rochester's Seneca Park Zoo with Deacon Kevin Carges Jan. 4

Deacon Carges is raising money for a surgery Shana needs due to wounds she suffered in a machete attack in her native Jamaica.

By Jennifer Burke/Catholic Courier

It's an unlikely friendship, but it's one that was meant to be. That's what Deacon Kevin Carges believes about his

76

friendship with 17-year-old Shana Campbell, who two years ago survived a horrific machete attack in Jamaica.

"People come into our lives for a reason, and I don't know why Shana came into mine," Deacon Carges said, noting that nonetheless, "God is working through Shana, and I know he has great plans for her."

The teen came into Deacon Carges' life in January 2015 after a conversation he had with Sharon Campbell Danvers, principal of Davis Primary School in Old Harbor, Jamaica. Deacon Carges had contacted the principal to tell her that the group he helped found, Eight 4 World Hope, had raised enough money to fund the first phase of a major project at her school. During the course of their conversation Danvers asked Deacon Carges to keep her cousin, Shana, in his prayers. When Deacon Carges casually asked why Shana needed prayers, Danvers explained that in September 2013 her cousin had been brutally attacked by her own machete-wielding father.

Shana survived the attack but was left with scars all over her body and a tracheal tube in her throat. In January 2015 she especially needed prayers because she was suffering from a serious infection in her tracheal tube and the hospital she'd been treated at in Jamaica was unable to provide any further help, Deacon Carges said.

"As I heard the story, it was overwhelming to me," recalled Deacon Carges, who serves at Our Lady of Peace Parish in Geneva.

He was moved to take action and reached out to several doctors that he knew sometimes worked in developing countries, but they all said the surgery Shana needed was too difficult for anyone they knew to perform.

"I then just wrote letters randomly to various doctors asking for someone to help me," Deacon Carges said.

He mailed out 30 letters and received just one response, from Dr. Richard Constantino, who practices internal medicine at Rochester General Hospital and belongs to St. Benedict Parish in Canandaigua. Constantino enlisted the help of a colleague, *otolaryngologist Dr. Robert Oliver, and together they began calling colleagues around the country in search of a doctor who could perform the complex surgery Shana needed.*

"It took months of searching but finally we got a doctor. Dr. Robert Lorenz at the Cleveland Clinic agreed to help," Deacon Carges said. "The surgery is estimated at $55,000, but after hearing Shana's story (the doctor and hospital) reduced the cost 35 percent to approximately $35,000."

Shana Campbell and Deacon Kevin Carges walk together during a visit to Seneca Park Zoo in Rochester Jan. 4. Deacon Carges has been helping the 17-year-old get the surgery she needs at the Cleveland Clinic.

Shana traveled to the United States in December 2015 to meet with her new doctors and spend Christmas with Deacon Carges' family. The doctors confirmed Shana is an excellent candidate for surgery, during which her surgeons will take a piece of her rib and insert it in her throat to cover the hole before placing a tube into her throat to open the airway, Deacon Carges said. The tube will be removed after five weeks, he added.

Deacon Carges currently is leading a fundraising campaign to raise enough money to cover the cost of Shana's surgery, as well as future plastic surgeries to fix her many scars from the machete attack, he said. So far, he's raised about $15,000, and while the campaign still has a long way to go, its success thus far has inspired Shana, who returned to Jamaica on Jan. 9.

"She is back home and happy to know so many people care about her. She had lost hope, and we have given that gift back to her," Deacon Carges said.

Deacon Carges downplays his own role in bringing hope back to Shana, and instead focuses on the gifts she's given to those who've been moved by her story and her courage. Shana doesn't say much because she has to hold her finger over the hole in her throat in order to speak, but she has a sweet, shy smile that instantly endears her to people, he said.

"She brings a smile wherever she goes. She has such a big heart. She's a beautiful soul, she really is," Deacon Carges said. "It's very clear to me God is working through her. When I started doing this I said, 'Well, I don't know what I can do.' I'm just a silly old guy, but God took over and started opening doors. God has a special plan for this one. I am blessed to be a part of it."

EDITOR'S NOTE: To contribute funds to be used for Shana's surgery, mail checks payable to Shana's Surgery Fund to Deacon Carges at 330 S. Main St., Canandaigua, NY 14424.

I was so excited to read the article and finally know that Shana's story was getting out there. I thanked God for opening this door for me and pressed on, seeking more doors to open. I now had two articles in hand as I spoke to people about Shana and my efforts to help her.

Unfortunately, the newspaper was distributed by geographic area of interest, not throughout the whole diocese, so it appeared only in the area of my own church in Geneva, New York. I did receive a few thousand more dollars in donations, but it could have been much more if everyone in the Diocese of Rochester had seen it. Again, I had to accept it as God's will, He had brought us this far and I knew I just had to keep trying, even though it seemed like such a challenge.

I will admit that I would often lie in bed just searching for ideas and praying to God to ask Him for guidance, for Him to open a door or shed some light, but, most of the time, I was left with darkness. It hurt and often made me sad that I was making such little progress. All I had to fall back on was the fact that Shana had already overcome so much; I was certain God had a special place for her in this world. She shouldn't have survived the attack, her government was turning deaf ears to her pleas for help but claimed they were still trying, she was scarred and left with a tracheal tube in her throat that would force her to deal with infections and issues the rest of her life—but she was ready to accept it if she had to. Yet, she was now part of my life and, since I had heard her story, it was a part of me. I thought when I heard her story there was nothing I could do besides pray for her.

I did pray for her, but God kept prompting me to try to do a little more: to seek, to ask, to act. Little did I know that it would lead to great hope when Dr. Constantino replied to my letter offering to help me. That hope would continue to grow when he, along with Dr. Oliver, would find Dr. Lorenz, who was willing to do the surgery at the Cleveland Clinic. Nor could I have even dreamed that the hospital would reduce the cost of the surgery by 35 percent and all I would need to do was raise a portion of the money. It was all perfect in my mind: God in action right in front of my eyes, and all I had to do was raise the needed funds, yet I was failing.

It had finally come together in May 2015 when the doctors and hospitals said they would help, but now it was the end of February 2016 and all I had was $18,000— not even a third of my goal after eight months. To make matters a little more difficult, a new estimate came in from the Cleveland Clinic after our visit in January, and they raised the cost an additional $7,000, due to the additional damage in Shana's throat that needed to be repaired.

THE CLEVELAND CLINIC FOUNDATION
ESTIMATE OF CHARGES

Patient Name: _SHANNA CAMPBELL_   CCF #: _8131-141-2_

Thank you for selecting The Cleveland Clinic Foundation as your Health Care Provider.
The following is the estimated cost for your service/surgery.

Procedure/Service: _Removal Laryngeal Lesion ; Skin Split Graft ; Direct_
Laryngoscopy ; Rib Cartilage Graft
Estimated Hospital Days: _5_   Physician: _Robert Lorenz_
Estimated Anesthesia/Operating Room Time: _5_   Hour(s)

Procedure 1	$ _5106.00_	CPT _31300_	
2	$ _3214.00_	CPT _15100_	
3	$ _868.00_	CPT _31535_	
4	$ _3650.00_	CPT _21230_	
Surgery Total	$ _12,838.00_		
Prof Anesthesia	$ _2834.00_		
Physician Misc	$ _2500.00_		
Operating Room	$ _27,000.00_		
Tech Anesthesia	$ _3257.00_	Units: _20_	
Semi Private Room	$ _8495.00_		
ICU/Recovery Room	$		
Hospital Misc.	$ _4750.00_		
Total Surgery Estimate	$ _61,724.00_		

Pre-op Testing
      Prof Fees $ _____
      Tech Fees $ _____
Other $ _____ for _____

This is the Foundation's estimated cost for the standard procedure(s) described above. As
with any estimate, your charges may vary based on the actual service you receive. You
may be responsible for any additional services or increases in charges in order to provide
you with the highest quality services.

Please contact your insurance company directly to determine your benefit coverage. This
coverage will vary depending upon your individual insurance policy.

If you have any further questions, please do not hesitate to contact me.

Financial Counselor _BRUCE HEIL_   Date _1-15-16_
Telephone Number _216 444-4541_

ESTIMATE WAS UPDATED AFTER RECEIVING ADDITIONAL
PROCEDURE CODES FROM DR. LORENZ.

81

God Shows the Way

The news hit me while I was down and suffering from a loss of confidence. I had nowhere to turn but God. I prayed and asked God for help and guidance, for Him to show me a way. I felt guilty that I had been so confident—apparently overconfident—thinking that I could raise the money easily. It was a lesson in humility for sure. I should have known better than to think that I could just do this, thinking that everyone would hear Shana's story and that it would immediately make them help after touching their hearts like it did mine. I was wrong, plain and simple.

It was a harsh reminder that God's work is not easy, and that we will sometimes suffer in different ways while we minister and carry out our mission to serve. My suffering was internal, in my mind and heart. Shana coming to America was wonderful, and I came to realize what a great person she really is. I could understand how God was taking special care of her because she had such a beautiful heart with so much to offer the world.

By March I was feeling lost, not sure where to go or how to get something going. No news organization would even respond to me, I had asked all my friends and family, and I certainly could not afford to personally take on the cost burden. I prayed. It was the only thing I could do, nowhere else to go but to God and ask for help.

About a week later, I got a call from one of my parishioners at Our Lady of Peace, Joe Cirencione, the chair of the annual St. Joseph's Table Dinner. He had seen the article in the Catholic Courier about Shana the previous month and wanted me to speak at the dinner about her. They would take up a collection at the dinner as well as hold a 50/50 raffle to help her out. I agreed, figuring that every bit helps and that maybe I could get a few hundred dollars. I had to preach that weekend in Ovid and Trumansburg, about an hour-and-a-half-long drive from my home. I was preaching on behalf of Catholic Relief Services. Although I enjoy preaching it tired me out speaking at all the Masses at a church on those weekends. By the time I got home, I had about an hour to rest and then head over to the dinner in Geneva. It was a long day, but I was excited to have dinner with my parish community and have the chance to tell Shana's story.

The dinner was wonderful and I shared Shana's story for about five minutes. I had nothing prepared; I just let my heart do the talking. The rest of the night was fun, and I had a great time talking and being with my parish community. Then Joe stood up and announced they had collected the largest amount in the history of the dinner. My eyes widened in surprise as he continued on; we received over $2,100 towards helping Shana this evening! I was shocked, and I immediately became emotional for a variety of reasons: I was tired, I was hurting from my lack of success, and I was searching for answers and ways to help not knowing where to turn. To get such a generous donation from my community really lifted my spirits. I felt like God was reaching out to me and answering a prayer—as if He were saying, "You're not alone, you never were."

As the dinner broke up and people started to head home, my friend, Judy Savaria, told me that Father Jim Hewes wanted to meet me. I had heard his name but we had never met. I excused myself and walked over to him and introduced myself. Apparently, Father Jim was very big into ministering to people in the developing world, especially in the Philippines, where he served the people who lived in one of the many landfills there.

He went on to ask me several questions about Shana and my efforts to help her, after which he told me that he would like to help me further. He had raised approximately $350,000 for the people in the landfill after hearing about how hundreds of people were killed in an accident when a seven-story pile of garbage fell on their homes. He was moved to action by this and had devoted much of his free time towards it.

After seeing my emotional thank you for the community donation, he wanted to get involved and said he could help. He liked that there was a specific goal and a specific result. It was clearly the story of the starfish in his eyes, as it had been in mine all along as well:

Basically that story is about a young boy walking along a beach and tossing random starfish back into the water after a large storm had washed many up on the beach. While many were dying in the hot sun, the boy was literally saving a few by throwing them back into the surf. When challenged by an older man about why he even bothers and asking what difference it will make, the boy tosses another in the water and reminds the gentleman that it makes all the difference to that one.

Father Jim got to work that evening. He called me shortly afterward and told me that he was reaching out to some of his friends for donations. He had also contacted a friend of his at the Democrat and Chronicle, the largest newspaper in the city of Rochester, and suggested they do a story about Shana. I told him I had tried that but had no success. He insisted and said that his friends who worked there would help.

I was hopeful but I had my doubts. One person in the media business told me that it would be difficult to get coverage for Shana's story because she isn't local, and they want stories about local people. Father Jim emailed me later, writing that his reporter-friend would think about it, but didn't want to start a precedent, otherwise everyone seeking help for someone in need would ask for a story in the paper. I could understand that—there is so much need in this world—but I prayed that it would still happen for Shana.

The next day I heard that the reporter decided not to do the article, but instead would refer the story to a fellow reporter who did a column called Pay It Forward. Within the week, reporter, Erica Bryant, called me and we talked about Shana and her situation. She did a wonderful job reaching out to Dr. Lorenz at the Cleveland Clinic and to Shana herself, now back in Jamaica. After a few phone calls and emails, she wrote the article and it appeared on Holy Saturday, the day between Good Friday and Easter. It was a perfect symbol of how all hope was lost for Shana in her mind but, through the kindness of strangers reaching out to someone in need, we can find hope. Together we have given hope back to the one who had lost it all. It was a perfect Easter sermon being lived out, from darkness to light.

Deacon aids Jamaican girl
attacked with machete

Erica Bryant
Rochester Democrat and Chronicle

Shana Campbell survived a brutal machete attack in Jamaica. Deacon Kevin Carges of Our Lady of Peace Church in Geneva is trying to raise money for surgery that could repair a hole in her throat.(Photo: Provided photo)

Shana Campbell, a pretty young lady from Jamaica, cannot speak without using her finger to cover a hole in her throat. She received a tracheotomy two years ago after she was brutally attacked by a man wielding a machete. Her gruesome wounds were made even more painful by the fact that the attacker was her own father.

The tracheotomy — a surgical incision in the throat — saved Campbell's life, but left her with a variety of complications. It is difficult for her to speak, breathe and eat, and there is always the danger of infection. She cannot swim, which had been one of her favorite activities. When people talk to her, they look at the hole instead of her eyes.

Deacon Kevin Carges of Our Lady of Peace Church in Geneva has been raising money for a surgery that would repair her throat and improve her quality of life. He learned of her plight while checking in on one of the Jamaican schools that he supports through his nonprofit organization Eight 4 World Hope. The principal of the school is Campbell's cousin, and took custody of her after the attack.

Carges was haunted by Campbell's story. "It was so horrific it was hard to imagine," he said. "I thought about it and prayed about it and felt that I had to try to help."

Campbell visited Deacon Kevin Carges and his family over the Christmas holiday. (Photo: provided photo)

He has since raised $20,000 for a surgery that costs about $55,000. The surgery would be done at the Cleveland Clinic, which has agreed to reduce the cost by 35 percent to make it more affordable. Some support has come from Our Lady of Peace church and friends. In the local Roman Catholic community, some are connecting Shana's story to the Easter season.

"It seems to me that Shana has already gone through her own 'Good Friday' of suffering and dying," said the Rev. Jim Hewes, a retired priest. "Now we have a chance to help bring 'Easter' life into her by this restorative surgery."

Campbell, who just turned 18, traveled to Farmington, Ontario County, to spend the Christmas holidays with Carges and his wife, Jackie, daughter, Katy, and son, Andrew. They visited the Cleveland Clinic for a medical consultation and did things like visit the Seneca Park Zoo and attend a Rochester Amerks game.

Campbell enjoyed shopping and going to restaurants. Her favorite American dish was Applebee's spiced chicken with a strawberry milkshake.

The trip gave her hope, she said by email. "America is so much more than I expected." She was happy to meet some of the people who have heard of her story and are trying to help her. "I am touched that so many people have reached out," she wrote.

Campbell would like to pursue a career in medicine. Her favorite things to do are running and swimming — impossible to do since the attack. Going to the beach would be one of her first activities if the hole in her neck were repaired.

She is still struggling with the aftermath of the attack and her feelings that she could have somehow prevented it. "She thinks she must have done something wrong and maybe God is punishing her," Carges said.

The Jamaica Observer reported that Wayne Campbell had been angry that his daughter had reported his attempt to sexually assault her. To take revenge, he stabbed her in the neck and stomach. Police had to shoot Campbell's father in order to rescue her.

"The fact the she survived this attack at all is a miracle," said Carges, who wants Campbell to write a book that will inspire others to overcome their struggles. "I know God has big plans for her."

Shana Campbell traveled to the Cleveland Clinic to meet with Dr. Robert Lorenz concerning the possibility of repairing the hole in her throat. (Photo: Provided photo)

89

People who want to donate toward the cost of surgery can contribute by writing checks to Shana's Surgery Fund, 330 S. Main St., Canandaigua, NY 14424. There is also an online fundraising site at crowdrise.com/shanassurgery, but Carges suggests that people might prefer to send checks because part of your donation gets eaten up by fees when you donate online.

Erica Bryant is the Pay It Forward Columnist. Contact her at EBRYANT@Gannett.com.

The article worked wonders in spreading Shana's story, and people responded. I quickly received close to 300 letters expressing their love and prayers for Shana as well as donations ranging from $1 to $1,000. Combined with Father Jim Hewes' friends' fundraising, I reached the goal needed to do Shana's surgery by early April, slightly surpassing the $55,000 goal.

Father Jim told me that he almost didn't go to that dinner in Geneva, but something told him that he should. In retrospect, he thinks that it was God calling him to go there and meet me. From my perspective, it was God answering my prayers for help. In any event, we met and together we helped lift a starfish off the ground and throw her back in the water. It's funny, I kept telling Shana I was going to make her a star by telling her story to everyone— now she's getting closer; she's become at least a starfish.

THE PATH TURNS ROCKY

Shana's first surgery was scheduled for June 8, 2016, at the Cleveland Clinic. Of course, before any big surgery, there is the pre-op appointment to go over the procedure and do some tests to make sure everything can move forward. So, Shana and Sharon flew up from Jamaica, and the three of us met with Dr. Lorenz at his office the day before the surgery.

We were given our folder with everything we needed to know about the Cleveland Clinic and instructions as we arrived at the hospital.

Shana knew that the doctor would put the scope up her nose—she hated it but was ready for it anyway. As

Dr. Lorenz viewed her esophagus this time, he noticed something different: Her vocal cords were moving and responding as she did what was asked of her. He looked at me and told me he was much more encouraged after this viewing. "Her vocal cords are responding when I ask her to talk. I think I can save them, giving her a voice as well as healing her trach hole."

It was the best news we could have gotten. We might be able to give Shana back her voice as well as heal the hole in her neck. It was as if God had been listening to my prayers and answered them right there. I'll never forget the look on Shana's face when he gave us the choice of her voice or the hole in her neck being closed, but not both. Now to hear this was truly another gift from God.

Dr. Lorenz went on to explain how this was great news on a couple different fronts, as well. We would no longer need to take a piece of her rib to place into her throat for healing, nor would we need to place a tube into her throat that would hold things in place while everything healed. The ring that would have been placed in her vocal cords to keep them open so she could breathe would not be necessary any longer, since they seemed to close and open on their own. On top of all that good news, the whole procedure would be less expensive since it was less invasive.

The doctor had a few ideas on how to approach this procedure, and he wanted to have some leeway once the surgery began. When he began operating, he would determine the best course of action. We were all thrilled with the news and left the doctor's office crying tears of joy, praising God, and hugging each other.

We arrived at the surgical center at 8 a.m. the next morning. We were told the surgery would last anywhere from four to six hours, depending on what Dr. Lorenz decided to do. As we went through the process of registration, everything flowed as smoothly as you could expect. I had to run over to the Global Financial Services area and pay the estimated cost of surgery, which totaled $31,000, far less than the $40,000 I was prepared for, thanks to the changes in procedure. I walked back to the surgical area thinking about how God was taking such good care of Shana and how blessed I was to play a role in God's work helping someone in need. I was so excited for everything and I knew Dr. Lorenz would take great care of her.

After an hour or so, we were called into the pre-operating area to begin getting ready. Shana changed into the surgical gown and a nurse hooked her up to an IV. All of her vitals were measured and everything seemed good to go. It was just a matter of waiting for the surgery to commence.

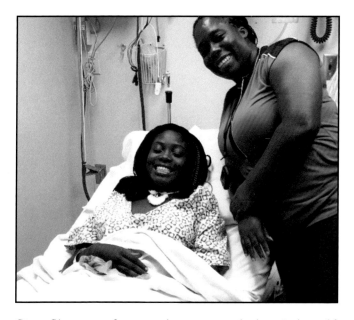

Since Shana was from another country, the hospital would allow someone to be with her all the way into the room where the surgery would take place. Sharon looked at me and said that I should go. I put up a weak fight but then readily agreed. I was handed a blue suit to put on to cover me up and keep the area sterile. It was so big that the three of us had to laugh at my appearance. I was glad for the laughs—they eased some of the anxiety about the upcoming procedure.

We were all excited for the surgery that would begin the healing process for real after so many months of talk and prayer. We prayed together before the surgery and I gave Shana a kiss on the forehead and said that I'd see her soon as we shared a smile.

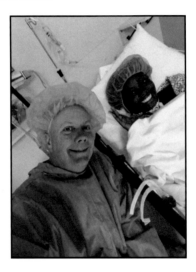

I walked out of the surgical room with tears in my eyes, realizing how far God had brought us on this journey. All of my doubts, moments of discouragement, and fears of letting Shana down were washed away knowing that it was all actually happening.

All I could do was pray to God, giving Him thanks for all that He had done for Shana. I was in awe of how God had used me to help her. I remembered hearing her story and thinking that there was nothing I could do to help. I didn't know who or where to turn to in the medical field, I had no money, and I didn't even know Shana. Back then, she was just a story, a very sad story that touched my heart. I thought about that during her procedure. There's so much evil in the world, yet God doesn't abandon us, ever! I thought about how He could use someone like me who had basically nothing to offer and yet accomplish something so great. I reflected on how I was an instrument of God, how he used me and guided me all along the way, how doors opened out of nowhere, and how people just showed up out of the blue often times willing to help and be a part of this journey.

What if I hadn't tried? It would have been so much easier to just pray for her, but sometimes we need to do more, we need to act. Even as I sought help, I felt defeated in my own mind, that there was nothing I could do. Who in their right mind would just start writing letters to random doctors seeking help? What are the chances of one getting a positive response? Dr. Constantino was sent to me from God; he helped me overcome the inevitable obstacles as we got medical files from Jamaica, enlisted Dr. Oliver's help in finding a surgeon skilled enough to help the traumatic injuries Shana had suffered, and searched all over the country until we found Dr. Lorenz.

The fact that the Cleveland Clinic discounted their services 35 percent also seemed to be a gift from God, as did that donors shared their money to help another person they did not even know, donating thousands of dollars from all over the area. It was all coming together right now as I walked down the hall back to that waiting area. I was overwhelmed at God's love for us and that he allowed me to be a small piece of helping her. I'll admit it, I cried for a minute as it all came rushing at me.

I knew nothing about the medical field, had no one to turn to for help, and I didn't know how to raise the money for everything that was needed, but in the end, it didn't matter because God had everything prepared and ready for Shana. All He needed was my "yes" to get things started. Even though I was filled with doubts regarding what I could do for her, it didn't matter. God was in control and He showed me just how well prayer and faith in Him can work.

The surgery lasted close to five hours, after which Dr. Lorenz came out to talk with Sharon and myself. By all accounts things went extremely well. The doctor had decided it was best to extract two inches of Shana's tracheal tube that were severely damaged, then lift the remaining part up and reattach it just below her vocal cords. This allowed the vocal cords to remain functional, and it removed much of the scarring that had closed off her airway passage and necessitated the tracheal tube. It was a painful procedure and required a stay of five days in the hospital.

Two tubes were inserted into each side of Shana's neck to drain blood from the surgery area while a new tracheal tube was inserted to allow breathing while the healing took place. She had a feeding tube since she couldn't swallow, and the hospital kept the air humidified for her to breathe to keep her throat moist as it healed. She was in rough shape and her pain level was high. It was hard to see that smiling beautiful face hurting so much, but we knew it was part of the journey toward being free of her tracheal tube.

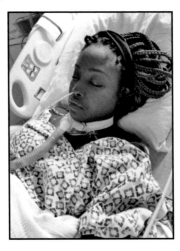

Dr. Lorenz was very happy with the procedure, and now all we could do was wait and allow her body to heal and recuperate from the surgery. If everything healed well, we could look at removing the tracheal tube on July 13th (her next surgical appointment) and done with everything.

That first night, it was difficult for Sharon and me to watch Shana suffer so much from the pain, but we knew it would be for the best. Several nurses checked on her constantly and made sure that all the tubes and medicines were administered properly. As the pain medicine wore off, she would wake and cry. I can't even imagine having a section of my throat cut out and reattached.

As the first day slowly became the second and then the third, Shana improved each day. Slowly, tubes and monitors were removed bit by bit, but the pain was still intense. By day three she could start to communicate a bit more. I would bring paper from my hotel room with a pen so she could write messages to me.

Late one night after a rough day, Shana motioned to me for the pad of paper. I knew she was hurting as an occasional tear would stream down her cheek.

It was difficult to read as she shared just how bad she felt. I leaned over and kissed her on the head and reminded her how brave she was and how proud I was of her. She had to fight, and I would be there for her throughout the journey.

By the next morning, she seemed to turn the corner. Her mood was better and she even cracked a small smile. It was good to see. Two days later we left the hospital. It was June 12th. I remember that because it was my birthday, and it was a great present to finally be going home. I was tired of the hospital and so happy that Shana was getting out, and I really missed my own family. I just wanted to hug my wife, Jackie, and tell her that I love her.

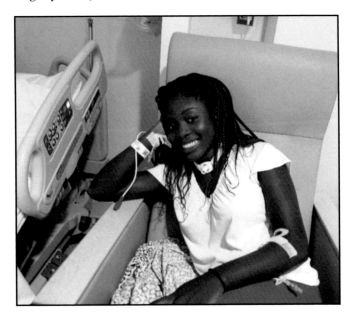

The doctor equipped Shana with a new tracheal tube as her throat healed. She still needed the tube due to the extensive swelling in her throat from the surgery, but we were told that it would dissipate over the next couple weeks. It was great to see Shana up and sitting in her normal clothing and showing off that beautiful smile again.

The new tracheal tube had a special feature that would allow her to cap it closed after her throat had healed enough.

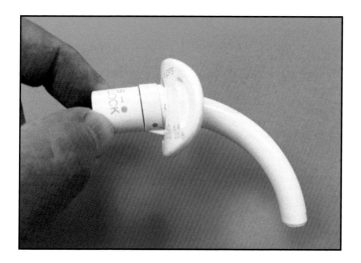

Here is a picture I took of a typical tracheal tube. It goes through the hole in Shana's throat and down the airway, bypassing all the damaged tissue in her throat.

Over the next couple weeks, Shana's pain dissipated and she began to show off her beautiful smile again. It was good to see her enjoying life again with less pain. The worst was behind her now—all she needed was the swelling in her neck to decrease so that her air passage would open. This would also allow her to begin talking again as air would pass by her vocal cords. We drove home excited for her future, but after a few days and then a week, her voice didn't come back. While it wasn't expected to return within the first week or so fully, surely after more than two weeks, we should have been able to hear something.

Shana would write or hope we could read her lips as she tried to express herself, but the voice we waited for never came. We went back to see Dr. Lorenz on June 29th for a follow-up visit to assess her healing. After the exam, he discovered that the swelling in her throat had not decreased as much as hoped—in fact, it hadn't decreased much at all. That was why Shana couldn't talk. Her airway was still blocked with swollen and scarred tissue from the surgery. In fact, the swollen tissue was actually beginning to heal together, sealing off what was once open after the surgery.

Dr. Lorenz called me the following day and decided that Shana should begin a steroid treatment immediately to help reduce the swelling. He also wanted to move the scheduled surgery up one week to July 7th. He went on to explain that everybody is different and reacts differently to various procedures. Shana's swollen tissue wasn't shrinking fast enough and needed a little help. The steroids would help and what he would do was go back into her throat with a balloon and "push" the swollen tissue back to the side, thus reopening the airway and allowing her to breathe and hopefully speak. It was a fairly simple procedure and would take no longer than thirty to forty minutes; she would be released from the hospital the same day.

Sharon flew up again for the procedure on July 7th. We anticipated the best result: Shana breathing through her mouth and talking again. Again, we went through the pre-operation procedures hoping for the best.

About an hour after the pre-op, Dr. Lorenz came down to talk with us and brought some pictures along to show us what was done. The before pictures clearly showed that Shana's throat had filled with swollen tissue and was indeed healing together, effectively closing the air passage.

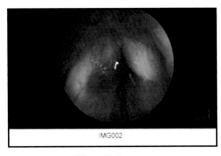

Closed Airway

100

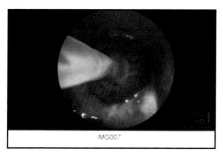

A balloon was inserted and the results were a
very clear open air passage.

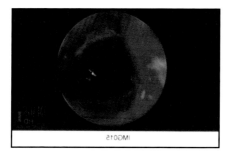

Opened airway after balloon.

Photos provided by Dr. Lorenz and the Cleveland Clinic

We were able to visit Shana for about ten minutes in recovery. She was very sleepy still but was coming around from the anesthesia. We were excited as we expected her to be breathing through her mouth and speaking slightly. She smiled, recognizing that we were there, and tried to speak, but she struggled. Sharon coaxed her on and then she spoke, "Thank you Jesus". Her voice was clear and stronger than I had ever heard before and she was breathing without the use of the tracheal tube. We were thrilled and overjoyed. Unfortunately our joy began to fade right before our eyes she began to struggle again. She was able to breathe through her mouth and the nurse said her vocal cords and throat were very sore from the surgery. She mustered a few muttered sounds, but her breathing became more labored as we stood there with her. The nurse asked us to leave, and about two hours later, we were called by the doctor and told that she could not breathe through her mouth. Her airway had swollen closed again. This was unprecedented and Dr. Lorenz was dumbfounded by it. Her tissue was very aggressive and would require a different approach.

Some friends of Sharon in Cleveland picked her up at the hospital while Shana and I headed back to Rochester. It was a solemn ride home. What was to be a joyous day with Shana breathing through her mouth and nose and starting to talk had turned into a situation where we felt like we were back to where we started. In reality, it wasn't quite that bad, it was just that our hopes had been dashed against the rocks. We didn't know what a different approach meant to Dr. Lorenz, although he had mentioned a few thoughts.

I felt bad for Dr. Lorenz. He is such a good man, on top of being one of the best surgeons in the world when it comes to things like this. It was clear through our various appointments and surgeries that he really cared about Shana and that he took it personally when the results weren't what we had hoped for.

Dr. Lorenz asked us to come back the following week to meet with him and his team. He would scope Shana's throat then, tell us what he was seeing and share his thoughts and suggested actions.

When we returned on July 13th, Dr. Lorenz told Shana that he was thinking about her much of the weekend. While Shana might not have picked up on that, I certainly did and it comforted me. He cared about her just like I did, and I knew that he would win out and find a way to heal her. He went on to tell us that he had met with his surgical team, and they went through many scenarios examining what might have caused the aggressive swelling in her throat. They considered allergies, reactions to medicines, and human error during the procedure, but there were no new solutions. Everything had been done to the best of their abilities.

The doctor went on to tell us that he had decided the best option would be to insert a "T-tube" into Shana's throat. They would do the balloon procedure like last time, but this time they would take the additional step and place this T-tube into her throat. The bottom of the "T" would exit the hole in her throat while the upper part of the tube would go from just below the tracheal hole up her throat through her vocal cords. Having a tube through her vocal cords would not allow her to talk, and it would cause pain and difficulty with swallowing foods and liquids in particular.

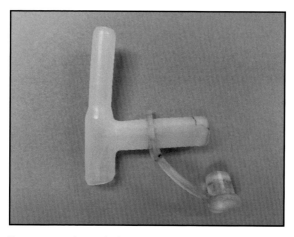

Dr. Lorenz explained that he thought the swollen tissue would be forced around the tube, leaving an airway open. We would leave the tube in her throat for two to four weeks and hopefully the tissue would heal around the tube. Dr. Lorenz felt that, after this timeframe, the tube could be removed and the tissue should stay as is, leaving her with an open airway. Once it was removed, Shana should be able to breathe through her mouth and nose and, finally, talk.

A SAINTLY INTERCESSION

The surgery was scheduled for the following day, and we left hopeful as it seemed like a good idea and it made sense. This was now going to be Shana's third surgery, one that was not expected. I was given an estimate that it would cost $10,000-$15,000.

The difficult part financially was that I was given an estimate before each surgery, but the actual bill would follow about thirty days later. I would have to cover the lower cost of each estimate, and the hospital and I would settle up afterwards. The estimate for Shana's first surgery was $31,000, for which I had to write a check literally twenty minutes before her surgery or they would've canceled the procedure. In fact, I was in the operating room with Shana when the room phone rang, and the caller told Dr. Lorenz to not start the procedure yet as the hospital hadn't received payment. After I explained things to Dr. Lorenz, he said that he was moving forward anyhow, which was confirmed five minutes later with a second call saying that they had the check and funds verified.

The total cost of the first surgery was $31,019 and the second was $12,433. I had been hoping that the second would've been her last. Now we were facing a third surgery, which would be the same procedure as the second with the addition of placing the tube in her throat, and probably a fourth surgery to remove the tube. I was constantly going over the numbers in my mind while I worried about having enough money to cover the hospital procedures and all the extra expenses, including medicine, food, and travel. I had met my goal of raising $60,000, but now I was beginning to think I would fall short. I hadn't factored in the potential of complications being as great as they were.

Every once in a while, a donation would come in from someone who had read or heard about Shana and was just now in a position to help. Her story was one that stayed with people, and I was constantly asked how she was doing. It was heartwarming to know so many people cared and I thought that, if I put an additional appeal out there, people might help.

I was sitting there in the waiting room worrying and trying to think of how I could cover the additional expenses that would be coming. Suddenly, Sharon looked up from her phone and told me that many people were contacting her from Jamaica all at once. Apparently, the Child Development Agency had announced on the news in Jamaica that they had come forward to help support Shana with money for her surgery and various other needs. We were shocked as we had tried for the last year to secure funds to help her. We were constantly met with the answer "we are trying," but nothing ever materialized. Sharon had been trying for over two years. After many futile attempts, no returned phone calls, and Shana's eighteenth birthday (which meant that the government was no longer responsible for her), I had given up on them. My contempt for the government of Jamaica had grown over the year due to lack of response, but it reached a breaking point when they actually called me fifteen hours before Shana was set to come to America and spend Christmas with my family and told me that she could not come. I was told that, because she is a ward of the state of Jamaica, I had to get their permission before she could come to the United States.

I am not a person to get angry very easily, but I lost it when they told me that. "Are you kidding me? Where have you been for this girl in the last year? I've found a hospital and a doctor to help her, I've raised money for the surgery, I've set appointments with various doctors and specialists to help her when she visits, and you have done nothing for her as far as I can tell. You don't even have the courtesy to return my calls or emails as I work on this issue. Where have you been for the last six months? And now you call me the day before she is to come and start caring?" I was ranting and words were flying out of my mouth as my anger and pent-up frustrations were unleashed. I was furious and, when I finally stopped talking, I realized that I was on a speaker phone and that there had been four people listening to me carry on.

I finally settled down, but it still felt good to get that off my chest. Ms. Aubry Budhi, the head of the CDA, remained calm and said that they understood. She went on to say they would go ahead and allow Shana to come. They even offered to send someone along to travel with her, but I had already set everything up for the visit, including having my good friend Deacon Fred Toca meet her in Atlanta to help her to the connecting flight. I thanked her for that, but told them to save the money toward helping with the surgery expenses I would incur later. That was the last time I had spoken to the CDA.

Now suddenly, they were coming through in a moment of need. I thanked God for providing yet again. While I sat there worrying and trying to come up with solutions, God gave me the answer I needed right away. I guess He knew I couldn't take much more of this rollercoaster ride at the time.

The following day, Shana had the surgery, and Dr. Lorenz came back out and told us that everything went well. The tube was placed into her throat and we were able to head back home. We were all tired and worn but hopeful again.

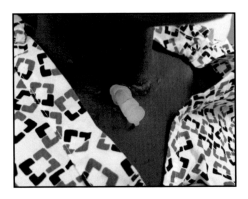

Not having the tracheal tube and necklace-like wrap around her neck showed much of what Shana had gone through on her neck: scars from the original attack, the first and second tracheal tubes, and the surgeries themselves. The doctor told us that fixing all the scar tissue would have to wait at least another year, but for now, we were just focusing on the inside of her throat. The tube should rectify the aggressive tissue swelling in her throat, thereby closing off her airway. All we could do was wait a couple weeks and pray that this worked. We were asked to come back July 26th for another appointment so we could make sure the tube was doing its job.

The first week was difficult for Shana as the tube going up her throat through her vocal cords was very uncomfortable. She had various pain medications and an inhaler to help her but it was still difficult. She struggled to swallow and was also feeling discouraged as she dealt with the various disappointments of the previous surgeries and the fact that there was no guarantee that this approach would work. Her issue was unprecedented and we had no idea what would happen once the tube was removed. I tried to be supportive and positive, but I was also anxious. I prayed for a positive outcome.

Two weeks later we headed back to the Cleveland Clinic for another appointment with Dr. Lorenz. By this time I was guarded against being too optimistic. I fully expected to be driving back home later that day and hoped to hear that things were healing properly. I wanted to hear Dr. Lorenz tell me that everything looked great and that we should come back in two more weeks to remove the tube. I felt in my mind that four weeks would be good and everything should be fully healed by then and her aggressive tissue in her throat would stop swelling.

The day started out rough when, at 8 a.m., I got a call from Dr. Lorenz's office and was asked if we could be there two and a half hours earlier than scheduled. I told them that it was impossible, but we would get there as soon as we could. Dr. Lorenz had to give a lecture at 3:00 p.m., and our appointment was overbooked at 3:30 p.m., unfortunately. It is almost a five-hour drive from my home to the clinic, so I woke Shana up and we hurried out the door. It was too important to miss an appointment and I was already anxious enough. I drove straight through and even got my first speeding ticket in fifteen years just before I got to Buffalo, but we made it in time.

We went through the usual procedure of the scope up Shana's nose to view her throat, vocal cords, and esophagus. Dr. Lorenz said that everything looked great! I exhaled as he told me the good news in relief, but he continued on saying that he would schedule surgery for tomorrow and remove the tube.

What? I wasn't ready for that. My mind was flooded with doubt: It was too soon, she needs more time, that damn tissue in her throat might swell again, we've gone through so much, let's wait a couple more weeks. The only words I could muster were "if you think it's best," but I was scared. I hadn't prepared myself mentally for another surgery right away. It would be her fourth in seven weeks.

I asked a few questions about the timing, but Dr. Lorenz felt confident and wanted to proceed. I knew how he had taken a special interest in Shana and wanted this to succeed, so I agreed even though I was worried.

That night I couldn't sleep because I was so anxious. The past disappointments haunted me. What if it fails, what will we do next? How much more time and suffering would Shana go through? How much more money will this all cost? These past two months had taken a toll on me and my family, I was just exhausted mentally, emotionally, and physically. It was hard watching Shana go through all this. I wanted to be certain, I wanted guarantees, but of course that was impossible. All I could do was pray and I did so much of the night as I lay in bed waiting for the 8 a.m. surgery.

After a while I felt much better, reminding myself how much God had taken care of Shana all along the way. We found a doctor and a hospital willing to help, we raised enough money and the doctor was confident he could help her. Finally the morning came and I met Shana and Sharon in the hotel lobby as we proceeded to the surgery unit.

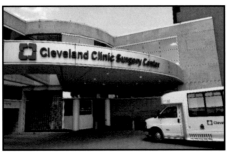

By now I knew exactly what to do as far as check-in and, everyone at the reception desk knew me. It was nice to be recognized but sad at the same time. All I could do was pray everything would work out.

We checked in and prepared for the surgery as usual. As with the other three times, I was allowed to go with Shana to the operating room. We always had about fifteen minutes or so together to talk about the surgery and how she was feeling. We would meet all the nurses and assisting doctors as they asked the same questions over and over to make sure they were doing the right thing to the right patient.

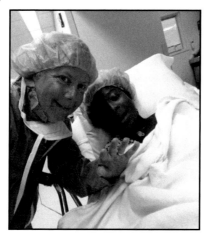

I took a picture of the both of us as I held up four fingers indicating that this was her fourth surgery. I thought it was funny but as you can see, Shana wasn't as excited

Eventually, Dr. Lorenz would walk in and everyone knew it was time to get serious and focus. Each time I said a prayer with Shana before she fell asleep from the anesthesia and then I would leave the room.

It was a long walk back to the waiting area each time. I thanked God each trip for taking such good care of Shana, helping me find a way to help her, healing her, and answering her prayers. I remember on this particular walk back thinking God could have made the path a little smoother, but that just isn't His way sometimes and there is often a reason for it that we can't see or understand in the moment. By the time I had reached Sharon in the waiting area, I was full of faith that God had everything in control and it would work out.

I was told that taking the tube out would be pretty quick, a matter of twenty or thirty minutes, and then Shana would go to recovery, where we could see her in about an hour. Like clockwork, the doctor called me thirty minutes after I had gotten to the waiting area and said that everything went great. He came down twenty-five minutes later to share a few pictures and tell us that he felt really good about things and that she should be breathing through her mouth and talking slightly. Her vocal cords were irritated from the tube, but in two to four weeks, her voice should return.

Sharon and I were so happy. Yes, it took a couple extra surgeries, but things looked like they would finally work out. The doctor put a tracheal tube back in her throat as a precaution, but it would be capped, forcing her to breathe through her mouth. I was so happy and couldn't wait to see her. We were told that we could see her in about an hour after the anesthesia wore off.

Well, an hour turned into three hours, and by this time all sorts of negativity had invaded my mind again. I just needed to see her and know she was all right. Finally, we got the call to come see her in Room 23. I knew right where it was—I had become far too familiar with the Cleveland Clinic and was even helping other people find their way around. Sharon and I quickly gathered our things and almost ran to the room.

We went into the room and saw Shana laying there in her bed sleeping. I sat in a chair facing the bed while Sharon walked up to her to give her a gentle nudge to wake her up. We wanted to hear her voice, to know that everything had worked out and she was healthy, but just being there was enough at the moment for me. Sharon spoke softly as she nudged Shana, trying to wake her gently. Shana eventually opened her eyes after a short while and saw Sharon as her eyes danced around the room. It always took a minute for her to recall what was happening and where she was when she awoke in the hospital room.

I stood up to join them at the bed as Sharon said, "Let me hear your voice, say something."

Shana opened her mouth but nothing came out. My eyes drifted down from her mouth and saw that her tracheal tube was uncapped. I asked her, "Can you breathe?" She nodded, yes. I continued, "I meant through your mouth." She tried as she covered her tracheal tube and shook her head, no. My heart sank as I began to think of reasons why.

I thought that perhaps the doctor still had to do something and that was why the tracheal tube was still uncapped. I searched for reasons and excuses but nothing convinced me as that dread began to set back in. I held her hand and smiled at her. All I could tell her was that I was proud of her for fighting so hard.

Her eyes closed and I sat back down, waiting for Dr. Lorenz to come in and talk to us. Sharon stood by Shana's side and continued to talk to her urging her to try and talk and breathe through her mouth. Sharon looked at me and could see how dejected I felt. I had no words, I didn't even know what to think as my expectations clearly were not met.

After about thirty minutes, Dr. Lorenz came in to check on Shana. He covered her tracheal tube with his hand and asked her to breathe, but she could not. He told her, "Your airway is clear, and if there is swelling, you need to force air through it."

He gave her a special cover for her tracheal tube that allowed air in, but not out. She could take deep breaths in, but she would have to force the air out through her mouth. Shana breathed in, but could not force the air out through her mouth. She would take the special cap off and let the air out through her throat.

I could see the disappointment on his face and all I could think was we took the T-tube out too early; we should have waited a couple more weeks.

Dr. Lorenz continued, "She has to force the air through, we can't let her leave the hospital like this. I have to do another procedure that should last about two hours. If she can't breathe out by then we will bring her back to surgery and reinsert the T-tube, then leave it in for three months." He looked at her and told her that he believed in her, and he knew that she could do it. He told me on the way out that this might just be all in her head since it has been years since she breathed like this. I went back into the room and talked to her, telling her how I believed in her, how she had come so far, that she had to fight, that she had to want this, she had to force the air through.

She took deep breaths and tried but nothing came out. I told her to rest a bit. We had a couple hours to do it, so she could just rest and try again in a bit. I sat down as Sharon got up to urge her on, but after fifteen minutes, Shana still wasn't able to breathe through her mouth. We all sat in silence as Shana continued to try on-and-off for the next hour. The nurse came in to check on her because Dr. Lorenz had called from the operating room to check on her.

After another thirty minutes of trying, Shana slowly pulled the sheets over her head and began to sob. She was giving up, and I had no words to help her. I was feeling defeated too. Sharon rose to stand next to her and comfort her. To hear her cry broke my heart, and I began to shed tears myself. The nurse came in and saw that Shana could still not breathe, so she called the operating room to begin preparing it for the surgery.

I sat there feeling helpless and dejected. I began to think about this whole journey since I had first heard Shana's story. How God had opened so many doors to get her here and, while it was rocky at times, God had guided us here and always brought us through. God was with her, with all of us, and He would not abandon her now.

I got up and asked Shana if I could pray with her. She nodded and put her hands together as I placed my hands on her head. I closed my eyes and prayed quietly in a low voice. I prayed to St. Blaise to intercede on Shana's behalf, to help her breathe and heal her throat. I asked him to please ask Jesus on Shana's behalf to help her, to allow God to work another miracle through his faithful servant St. Blaise. My prayer was desperate and faith-filled, and I knew if it was God's will, that it would be answered. I removed my hands and looked down at Shana with her hands still together in prayer. She looked up to me as I ended my prayer and I kissed her on the top of her head and walked out of the room. It was my last hope, to have God intercede on Shana's behalf.

St. Blaise is the patron saint to those suffering from throat ailments. In 316 AD, he was arrested for being a Christian. On his way to jail, a woman set her only son, who was choking to death on a fish bone, at his feet. Blaise cured the child and word of this miracle spread throughout the land. Today many churches, especially in Germany and Great Britain, are named after him. When I first heard Shana's story, it was to St. Blaise who I prayed to first, since her main injury was to her throat.

I walked out of the room and down the hallway. I just needed to walk, regroup, and prepare myself for what was to come. I needed to be strong and encouraging for Shana's sake. She needed that of me. I couldn't understand the "why" of God's plans sometimes, but I could accept what was happening. God loved Shana very much; I had witnessed so many things happen that allowed her to even get to this point. I knew that Dr. Lorenz would figure this out and she would be okay. It just might take longer than I hoped or expected. In fact, it already had, but this was God's work and timing, not mine. I reminded myself I am just His humble servant and am called to serve as a deacon. I must accept God's will and serve those in need. Shana was the one who needed me now.

As I headed back toward her room, I received a text from Sharon—all it said was, "Come back now!" I responded "ok" as I was walking that way already.

I wondered why she sent that to me and I thought maybe they were taking Shana back to surgery now. As I walked, I felt better about things, and I thought about our prayer to St. Blaise and began to thank Jesus for everything he had done for Shana. By the time I got to the room, only Shana was there. I walked in and she smiled at me with her eyes wide open. I looked at her and said, "You can breathe, can't you?"

She nodded and whispered, "Yes," simultaneously.

I hugged her tightly as she went on to say that Sharon had gone to look for me. Apparently, after I left, Shana had coughed violently, so loud in fact that the nurses from the nurses' station outside her room came running in, thinking that something had happened. Upon entering they found Shana breathing on her own without the tracheal tube.

In my mind, it was a miracle. I sat there holding Shana, thanking St. Blaise for his intercession on her behalf, Jesus for clearing her airway, and God for taking such special care of her. I admit it, I cried out of thankfulness. We were literally minutes away from rolling her back into the surgical room and inserting that T-tube back into her throat. God had answered our prayers. Others reading this can think what they like, but I know in my heart and mind that it was a miracle and a prayer answered by God through the intercession of St. Blaise. Nothing will ever make me think otherwise.

We went to church together the following weekend and I was so full of thanks and praise to Jesus for helping Shana. The community of Bay Knoll Seventh Day Adventist in Rochester and Our Lady of Peace in Geneva have been so wonderful and supportive. They always love to see Shana and everyone wants to hug her and tell her how she is in their prayers for healing and recovery. Their prayers are working and are very powerful. It is truly a blessing for me to see how much love and care Shana can garner with her story and beautiful heart from those who meet her.

FROM DARKNESS INTO LIGHT

We went back to Cleveland again for an appointment with Dr. Lorenz on August 17th. It had been two weeks since the last operation, and while Shana could breathe out perfectly fine, she was having some difficulty getting air in, so she continued to rely on her tracheal tube to breathe.

The examination found that, while everything had healed nicely, the airway near her vocal cords had closed slightly, reducing the amount of air she could get in and out comfortably. While she had healed enough to no longer need the tracheal tube and could in fact breathe on her own, this limited amount of air made her tire quickly and feel like someone suffering from asthma.

Dr. Lorenz suggested one more surgery that would be a quick in-and-out procedure. One more cut around the airway to increase its size where it had closed slightly and then an injection of steroids to keep the swelling down while the tissue healed. He felt that this would increase her breathing capacity by 30 percent.

It was clearly the right move to do but still discouraging: a fifth surgery with no guarantees and possible additional complications.

Shana didn't say much as we drove back home, but I knew she was feeling down. The next day I found her by herself crying. She eventually told me that, while each surgery held such great promise, each had been followed by disappointment as well.

What if this didn't correct her breathing enough to just have a normal life of physical activity? She wanted to run, swim, walk up stairs, and do whatever she wanted without having to stop and rest just to breathe.

What if her tissue swells again, what if the doctors make a mistake, what if …?

I understood what she was feeling and quite honestly - I was also pretty tired, but I reminded her how far God had brought her. We had to keep our faith and trust in God. All our prayers were being answered, and we just needed to continue with our praying.

It was her hope, trust, and faith in God that had delivered her to this point, and together we had witnessed prayers answered—if not real miracles. The fact that she survived the attack was her first miracle and God had not abandoned her.

So off to Cleveland Clinic we went again. This would be Shana's fifth surgery since the initial one on June 8th. All these trips and surgeries had taken their toll on us, but it was particularly hard for her. This surgery would happen above the vocal cords since her throat had healed well below. Dr. Lorenz said that perhaps he had been so focused on the major issue that he didn't give as much attention to the whole throat as he should have. This surgery would again be a "quick fix," lasting only about thirty minutes.

True to his word, the surgery was quick. Dr. Lorenz came down to talk to me afterward, letting me know that this should take care of everything and that Shana should be able to talk and breathe comfortably in two months. At that point she could finally remove the tracheal tube.

While I was happy to hear of the success of the surgery, I was honestly a little upset that we would have to wait an additional two months for her tracheal tube to be removed.

Shana had to return to Jamaica to start school again. In

fact, she should have returned already since school starts during the last week of August there. She would already return home late, missing two weeks due to this last surgery.

On September 6th, Shana returned home to Jamaica to begin school. I asked her what she was thinking after a week back in Jamaica. This is what she wrote:

After five surgeries, the doctor still said I had to keep this tracheal tube in for two more months. Oh my God, it was the worst of it all! I did not want to go back to Jamaica with the trach, that was the last thing I wanted. I would have to go back to school with it and the children would be asking me questions. My God, this summer has been so crazy. Moments of happiness and sadness and frustration. It was a lot. Now school. Seven subjects a day, and I'm so depressed at school. I want to give up at times but Kevin always says that things will be okay, be better. He is so optimistic all the time. The one thing I wanted to do was swim, and each time we visited the lake he would say, "Next time you will be able to swim," but it never happened during all four visits. He is always filled with hope but I have no patience. When I feel like giving up, I know Kevin won't give up, so I can't and won't either. Sometimes I think he doesn't deal with reality, but I have seen his frustration and disappointment as well. He and his family have helped me get this far and they love me and I love them. I have to keep fighting and put my faith in God. He has answered so many of my prayers already. Years ago, I had no hope, but now I have so much!

It was hard after four months to not have Shana around, but I knew that her being back home and in school was the best thing for her. She hadn't been to school in three years now and this was going to be a big adjustment with the added disappointment of not having the tracheal tube removed yet. A couple weeks later I got this message from her:

I feel like I am dying, I just can't do this, there is only so much *you can take. I'm just tired all the time, I just want out, I just don't fit here, I don't belong. Why did I come back to school in the first place? I feel some days like I am suffocating, I feel like I'm just not getting enough air. I feel like I am trapped and that I have died 100 times. It is so hot here, maybe I have died and gone to Hell. Yes, this is Hell, or maybe I just have issues. I don't know what is wrong with me but something is. I feel like I am in a different world sometimes, I don't hear the teachers. I don't know what I want, I thought this was what I wanted but obviously I was wrong, as always. Nothing makes sense, never did, I'm going crazy. Nobody knows what is going on with me, they don't seem to care. I know people care about me, but why do I feel so alone?*

The children at the school are all really nice but they ask me too many questions, there are so many of them. I feel like every single child has asked me. Eventually I just asked the principal to announce it so I could just stop being asked about it.

It was clear she was struggling on many fronts. There was little I could do but try to be her friend, remind her how much she was cared for by so many people, and that God loved her very much and would never abandon her. I wish we could understand or know God's plan for us, but sometimes we just have to maintain faith and hope until it is revealed.

It had been such a journey already since I heard her story filled with so many ups and downs. It was a struggle and tiring in every aspect of life. It was very much a cross the two of us were carrying together, but she had the majority of the weight.

I understood some of what she was feeling, the disappointment of sending her back to Jamaica for school with a tracheal tube still protruding out of her neck. It wasn't supposed to be this difficult, yet it was.

So many times I could feel that darkness creeping into my own thoughts since Shana came into my life with her story. Worry, fear, doubts, what ifs, they were always lurking, always there just waiting to pounce. As I reflected on the journey, it was clear that God was there, as well. Even my speeding ticket was reduced to a $20 fine and no points after I explained the story to the judge.

While events hadn't gone according to plan, my plan, it was certainly going according to God's, no doubt. To be honest, I didn't like His plan as well as mine, but He knew much better than I did, so all I could do was trust in Him and wait two more months as Shana's throat healed.

So we waited, hoping that her breathing would improve after the swelling in her throat receded. Five surgeries takes a toll and all those procedures required some serious healing time. After two months, she should be breathing better and she could find a doctor in Jamaica to remove the tracheal tube, a fairly simple procedure we hoped.

Two months went by with little improvement. While she could breathe on her own and even talk, anything additional like walking up stairs or any exertion would leave her gasping for air. We had come so far, yet not quite far enough to remove the trach.

We battled discouragement and wondered if this was the best it would get. While we originally thought two surgeries would correct everything, five surgeries later we still weren't at a point she could remove the trach comfortably. Then to top things off, she got another throat infection and experienced breathing issues twice. The doctors in Jamaica didn't know how to help her after such a complex operation. They did their best to treat her and eventually she would feel better, but it took a toll on her mentally and emotionally as well as physically. She was so close, yet still so far.

We brought her back to Rochester that next January and took her to Dr. Oliver because he was local. There was still some blockage that he felt could be removed. His message was difficult to hear, but also good in the fact that maybe we could still improve upon her condition.

Unfortunately, there was no time for a surgery at this time because Shana had to return to Jamaica for school as well as visa issues, but we could try in the summer.

Having finished her school year in July 2017, Shana came back to the states in hopes of doing one more surgery that might finish things off once and for all.

My hope was to have Dr. Oliver do the surgery because he was right in Rochester, and I was so tired of driving back and forth to Cleveland. Dr. Oliver was willing to help as we began the process of seeing if the local hospital might donate some of the services for the operation. My funds had dried up after five surgeries so I tried to raise more as well as beg for donations from the hospitals and staff.

After a couple months, we weren't getting very far and Shana was getting impatient waiting. I didn't blame her. I spoke to Dr. Oliver again and after he explained just how complex this sixth surgery would still be, he advised me that we really should have Dr. Lorenz do it since he is a specialist.

I realized at that moment how I misunderstood how complex her surgeries were. Dr. Oliver is an excellent surgeon with great skills, but for Shana's situation, he wanted her to have the best. Dr. Lorenz made the surgeries sound more simplified than they actually were, but he was an expert at this type of surgery. Maybe it was also me just being lazy and tired as well, hoping that everyone could accommodate me when I should have been doing things right to begin with and contacting Dr. Lorenz from the start.

I apologized to Shana. After all we had gone through, I had not held up my end of the bargain doing the best I could for her. I also apologized to Dr. Oliver for putting him into a difficult position. I called Dr. Lorenz as I should have done months ago with my tail between my legs hoping he would still help and not be offended that I went to someone else to help.

I think another part of it was he had already done so much to help us. He was great in every aspect and I was so thankful for him. When I called to ask if he would help one more time, he didn't hesitate to say yes. I told him I was getting low on money, but that wasn't an issue, he truly wanted to help Shana heal as much as possible.

We followed up with Dr. Lorenz on March 2nd, 2018. After his examination, her throat was in great shape, the airway was clear, the surgeries had been a complete success. The only remaining problem left were her actual vocal cords. They still had some scar tissue and weren't opening fully to allow air to pass in and out as much as we had hoped.

We scheduled a sixth surgery for the next day in which Dr. Lorenz would actually cut into her vocal cords and remove scar tissue. If the surgery were successful, Shana would be able to remove her tracheal tube in two months if she felt she could breathe without it.

We did the usual procedure and sent her off once again to the operating room. I made the long walk back to the waiting room by myself this time and sat alone. I reflected how God created the earth in six days and rested on the seventh. I prayed that this would be Shana's last surgery, and she would finally have rest from this ordeal. She was now 20 years old and had spent 25 percent of her life dealing with these aftereffects of an attack by her own father. I wondered how many surgeries she endured in Jamaica just to save her life. She had spent six months in the hospital just recovering from that. It was a miracle that she even survived that attack. How God must love her so much, and that He had plans for her still. He needed her in this world for some purpose, maybe just to share this story.

She has suffered enough, Lord. Please heal her and let her get on with her life of serving you whatever that may be, I prayed.

Almost on cue I got a call from the front desk that Dr. Lorenz had finished with the surgery and everything went well. He felt this would be the last one she needed and we could remove the tracheal tube for good in a couple months, if all went well with the healing.

Shana went back to the Bronx to stay with her Auntie Madge who had taken her into her home. The trach was only a precaution in case the healing didn't go as planned, but everything seemed to go well.

We stayed in touch as we hoped our prayers for healing would be granted. After a week she was already wearing a cap over her tracheal tube that prevented air from going in and out. It forced her to breathe only through her mouth and nose.

On June 20th, we drove back to Cleveland Clinic together to meet with Dr. Lorenz. Shana felt she was breathing better and her voice was much stronger than I had ever heard before. We were both filled with hope, yet scared that there might be another setback. It had been just over two months since the last surgery, and there was a chance Dr. Lorenz might suggest she remove the tracheal tube once and for all.

Dr. Lorenz greeted us with a smile and immediately began the examination. He removed Shana's tracheal tube and put the scope through the hole in her throat and began looking around. I was able to watch on a monitor what he was seeing. After a couple minutes, he said he felt she could remove the tracheal tube permanently. He placed some sterile strips over the hole in her throat along with a gauze bandage and then covered it with clear seal. Shana was finally breathing and talking without a tube in her throat!

I couldn't help but shed some tears out of joy and thanksgiving to so many. The faces of all the people who had stepped up to help me came rushing at me like a train: the doctors, friends, family, so many people who had helped.

I wanted to tell them all that we won, we overcame, we accomplished our goal, that Shana was going to be fine and be able to live the rest of her life without that tube sticking out of her throat.

It had seemed so impossible from the start, even more so as the complications and difficulties arose. Yet God always showed us a way to overcome every obstacle. It was just an incredible journey and I was so thankful to be part of it.

All that was left was for the hole in Shana's throat to close up and that would happen on its own over time. No more surgeries, no more doctor appointments, no more five-hour drives to Cleveland and subsequent rides back home. When all the bills finally settled out, we owed the Cleveland Clinic $1,421 after spending close to $140,000 for everything. I mentioned this to Dr. Lorenz, and he told me he would have the hospital make an adjustment so the ending balance was zero.

I was incredibly happy for Shana knowing through God's graces we had made a difference. We overcame an evil by simply extending ourselves to help another. Glory be to God.

EPILOGUE

I saw God reaching out to Shana through me and so many others, each bringing their own gifts along the way. It has been a journey where I witnessed God's presence in so many ways through so many people. It was filled with miracles, answered prayers, and literally seeing someone brought back into the light of a loving people.

I have been blessed by God to be His humble servant trying to do His will and work. I've learned through this journey that, while I may have gifts to share, I don't have them all. I could never have done any of this without so many others reaching out. I didn't do the surgeries, write the articles or come up with the needed funds. I just heard the story of someone who was hurting and tried to help.

When we come together, each of us bringing our God-given talents, abilities, and gifts, it is then that we see God's manifestation come to its fullest. It is why I had to share this story because it is exactly what happened here. This was punctuated as Eight 4 World Hope raised the needed $153,000 for Davis Primary School in just 3 years. It was fully funded addressing all the needs and expanding it to allow 1000 children to attend it in a safe and comfortable condition. While I doubted my own abilities upon first visiting the school, it was in simply trusting and having faith in God to work through us that we accomplished more than I could have dreamed.

My prayer is that each of you that reads this book will open your hearts to God and allow Him to work through you. If you allow that to happen, you will exceed what you might think you could accomplish if it is God's work. God's love and glory is far greater than we, as humans, can ever comprehend or understand. He has plans for each of us, plans we don't even know about yet, perhaps. If you are willing to give of yourself and carry that cross in service to others, prepare yourself for an awesome journey. You will encounter a joy that the world cannot offer.

Through this story I pray you realize it often won't be easy or go according to plan. Your plan may be different than God's plan, and we have to accept that. The ups and downs and the twists and turns we don't see coming are part of God's work. Have faith, my friend, and never give up for God will never abandon you, happy journeys.

God bless.
Kevin Carges
December 2018

Shana: "I wouldn't change a thing"

I have come to realize a lot of things these past years. One is I should learn to appreciate life, my life, more. Every time I think I am going through a lot, there is always someone worse off than me. I think we can all relate to that but even though I know this, I couldn't help feeling awful about myself, asking "why me" – but "why not me?" Jesus was without sin and He had to die for us, so who am I to say, "why not me?"

Everyone suffers in life, some greater than others. I guess it was just my turn. No one's life is perfect or fair. That is life, right? Out of all the bad things that happened to me, good has come out of it. I've gotten a chance at a better life.

I have grown so much in the past five years, not physically, but spiritually. I have become a better person, a happier person, a person who doesn't look at the negatives. I had been waiting so long to take my trache out, so long that I had accepted that I would just live with it, and now that it is out, I don't exactly feel different.

It feels strange and weird to some degree but no different other than I can talk and breathe better. I always thought I needed to take the trache out to feel normal, to live again. Although the trache restricted me from doing certain things, it never stopped me from being me. I realize that now, having gone through all this.

I guess it was all in my mind, thinking the removal of my trache would make me happy. It did in some ways, but I mean really being happy with myself and who I am, no trache, no evidence, no one else would have to know what I had been through. No more explaining why I had a trache, and I can hide the other scars on my belly. I would be fine, happy even, but the thing was I would be fixed physically, but not emotionally. I would always remember and know what I had been through even if no one else knew.

All I know now is I am so much better than I was a few years back. Sometimes I wonder if "not" removing my trache would have been easier. It would be so easy to be that timid, anti-social, depressed person again. Being happy is what is hard at times, not giving up is hard because there were so many reasons to do just that, to not go on and accept my fate. But I couldn't because so many others cared so much about me. There were hundreds of people who donated money to me even though they have never even met me. There were people who heard my story, cared about me and were willing to give of themselves to me, a mere stranger, someone they did not know. For whatever reason, some people feel they don't need anyone. I don't believe it is true, everyone needs someone or something for no man is an island. Perhaps you are better off with some people not in your life but it is because of those that did care about me that I had to keep moving forward. That is how I have been able to go on, God first, along with friends and family. I'm so thankful and happy the doctors and so many others didn't give up on me even when I wanted to.

My struggles and my story have definitely molded me into the person I am today, and I wouldn't change a thing. I pray my story will give you courage, strength and hope in your own struggles. It is all for the glory of God.

Shana Campbell
December 2018

About the Author

Deacon Kevin Carges grew up in Elmira, New York, until attending St. John Fisher College in Rochester, New York, in 1980 obtaining a bachelor of science degree in economics in 1984. He received a master's degree in pastoral studies from St. Bernard's School of Theology and Ministry in 2005 and was ordained to the Sacred Order of Deacon by His Excellency, the Most Reverend Matthew H. Clark, Bishop of the Diocese of Rochester New York. He joined Catholic Relief Services and became a Global Fellow Ambassador, preaching and speaking to groups around the United States in 2009. In 2010 he founded a non-profit group called Eight 4 World Hope to serve people in developing countries in conjunction with Food for the Poor. Its mission is to give hope to the voiceless, one community at a time, by providing a safe, stable, learning environment that fosters long-term opportunity for individuals and families. Carges is the father of four and grandfather of five. He has operated a printing and copying business in Canandaigua, New York, since 1995. He also has served as deacon at Our Lady of Peace Parish Community in Geneva, New York, since 2010.